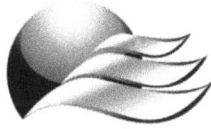

The Seventh Dimension of Leadership

Dr. Kathy E. Williams

Table of Contents

Acknowledgements

I am first and foremost forever grateful to my Savior Jesus
Christ for reaching into my life and extending salvation and grace.
The journey from acting out as an angry, rebellious drug-addicted
drop-out teen of the late 60's to this moment has been epic. I like
to say, "The journey has been rugged, but the scenery has been
memorable." My mother died of bone cancer on December 15,
2015. We both knew that she would not be here for the conclusion
of my journey, but her encouragement is an eternal flame in my
heart. My spiritual mentors are also gone from this earth but ever
present with their countless words of wisdom. God has blessed me
not only with four children, eight grandchildren and six great
grands (and counting) but an incredible number of Mommak kids.

While a single mother of three children, I completed high
school through night school classes. My chief ambition was to
secure a factory job. The roller coaster ride of layoffs, welfare,
and unemployment convinced me at the age of 36 to enroll in a
vocational college. My first work-study supervisor invited me to
lunch one day. After my supervisor ordered her meal, I told the
waiter, "I will have what she is having." Diane glared at me and
said, "How do you expect to make decisions about your life when
you cannot make decisions about your lunch." Whenever I stand

in front of a group to speak, I consistently relay to them that I am not there because of success but because of lessons learned from failure. After taking 18 years to finish a 4-year degree, I realized that it was not time to stop. Building on a master's degree in Strategic Management inspired me to begin the doctoral work.

Exegetical Analysis was in the first semester. I will never forget Dr. Corne' Bekker using the term *pericope*. I knew instantly that I was in over my head as I not only had never heard the word, but I could also not locate it in any common dictionary. Once I gathered that it meant "a passage of scripture" I naively took on the entire story of Abraham which more accurately qualifies as a "chunk of scripture." It is the difference between a slice of cake and a hunk of cake. It was if the professors lined up to take turns at pushing me toward goals I didn't even know I had and a depth that I thought certain was going to be the cause of my drowning.

Acknowledgment is more than a thank you. It is the inclusion of each person's contributions toward the journey that still lies ahead.

Preface

Why this book? Particularly in the United States, we are constantly reminded of the separation of church and state. As leaders in the 21st century, we must have a way to be spiritual while operating within secular systems. After finishing my four-year degree, I spent months in prayerful consideration concerning my choice of pursuing a ministry-focused degree while asking the question, "Will that degree translate well or be accepted in secular circles?" The other half of that internal debate was, "If I pursue a secular degree, will it transfer well into a ministry setting?" With both the master's at Indiana Wesleyan University and now the Doctorate of Strategic Leadership (DSL) from Regent University, I gained the perfect balance and the best of both worlds. Each university is rooted in Christian principles and has a vision of equipping leaders to be influential in the world. We are compelled to reframe our reference and shift from serving as Christian leaders to becoming leaders who are Christians. That is the outcome you will gain from reading this book. You will acquire insights and applicable skills that equip you, the reader, on the fine art of becoming a leader who is a Christian. The Bible is filled with *best practices* and *evidence-based practices* and other concepts that align to all the leadership trends for our contemporary society and global economy.

A ministry colleague said once, "We have to learn how to drink Coke from a champagne glass." She was expressing that we must develop a set of skills that puts us in circles of leadership without compromising our spiritual standards. As I was working on my four-year degree, the Lord blessed me to be one of five non-traditional students in the country to accept an award in the Library of Congress. After that accomplishment, I spent approximately 18 months traveling around the U.S. and speaking to adult education groups. It is a standard social protocol to host receptions and acknowledge keynote speakers. Those events typically include a bar. While I do not personally drink alcoholic beverages, that did not prevent me from ordering a soft drink and enjoying the networking and conversations. Our challenge is to master the biblical mandate to serve as ambassadors for Christ. Ambassadors are functional in other cultures without losing sight of their own citizenship. The patriarch Abraham is a classic example as his travels took him to 17 various locations. His first command was to leave his country and kindred (Genesis 12:1) and step toward an unknown destination. That was but an opening instruction for a way of life. It is often in our willingness to embrace uncertainty that our destiny is most clearly revealed.

Brief Interjection

During the 18 months of travel and speaking, I not only learned how to maneuver through an airport but how to tip and master various social protocols. While I was in Washington, D.C. to accept the award, I remember sitting on a bench eating a hot dog that I had ordered from a street vendor. I was extremely proud of my hot dog from a hot dog cart. During a trip to Seattle, I had the privilege of meeting Wilma Mankiller, the first woman Principal Chief of the Cherokee Nation. She and I sat off to the side during a reception and shared stories of our spiritual culture.

When it came to accept the award, the room was filled with Congressional representatives, CEO's and other business and educational executives. Every other person that gave a speech pulled out a manuscript and delivered a message of articulate perfection. When it was my turn, I stood up and pulled an index card out of my pocket. It had only a few words scribbled on one side. I said, "Where I come from, when God is good, we testify. I did not bring a speech with me. I brought a testimony."

During the trip to Washington, D.C. my youngest daughter and I visited the Smithsonian. One of the displays concerned the

Civil Rights era and had both water fountains and doorways that were marked "Whites" and "Colored." I was appalled that at the end of the 20th century, I watched a Caucasian child pull another child back from the "Colored" doorway and point to the other door saying, "This one is for us." How easily undone our progress can be!

My two greatest struggles in ministry are saying grace and closing a message. I have no legitimate explanation for the first, especially since I was raised in Catholicism where saying grace is mandatory. If any of you have seen *The Never Ending Story*, then you understand my struggle with closing a message. There is always one more point to be made, one more story to tell, one more character to explore. While I respect the scholarly wisdom of educated individuals, most of my mentors were elderly Black women with little to no formal education. In the African-American church, those women are respectfully and affectionately called church mothers. Mother Genevieve DeBow dropped nuggets like, "Ain't no shame in needing more prayer." Mother Mildred Boyd told me once, "You can be in the same tree, but it doesn't mean you have to sit on the same branch." Academia could use Mother DeBow's words to advocate for learning organizations and Mother Boyd's words to explore diversity.

During a time when I thought someone was being grossly unfair to me, Mother DeBow said, "Sometimes God is showing you what NOT to do." Mother Clotilde Jones told me, "If you learn one thing in your life, you better learn how to pray. Call on His name, because the name of Jesus can do anything." When one of the church mothers became ill, several of the women from church took turns sitting with her. I loved taking my turn as she told me stories about what it was like to be a Christian during World War I and how she had to decide about whether to work overtime or go to church. I loved the stories of the old people. Through the many church mothers, I learned how to pray, study the Word, fast, and trust that Jesus is the answer to every question, the peace in every storm, and the miracle for every struggle.

This book first and foremost brings life experience and practical knowledge that are illustrated by stories. Supporting those elements is a vast amount of scholarly research and words from the experts. The heart of ministry for me has always been at the people level. I love street preaching and outdoor tent revivals. I love jail and prison ministry and going to rehabilitation centers. I especially love ministering to people that others have determined are hopeless. When a person is at the bottom of the barrel, the only direction left is up. If life has not been difficult for you, I am the loudest voice cheering for your opportunities. But if you are one that knows about failure and recovery then we share spiritual DNA. I love practical ministry. Can you make use of what is offered? How is your day-to-day life impacted by the messages from the scripture? What does God want us to do? Whatever circumstance comes my way, I have learned to ask, "God, what do you want me to learn from this that I could not have learned any other way?" My prayer is that this book becomes part of your never-ending story by opening your mind and your heart to considering some fresh perspectives of the dispensations and the woman at the well as they relate to leadership.

Introduction

Why give yet another book on leadership any attention at all? Why go past the first page of this book? Surely there is enough literature to keep any dedicated leader reading for the rest of their career. Recently, when I opened my iTunes, it offered an upgrade. We think nothing of receiving such offers in our technology-driven world. Seeing a new version does not cause me to think, "Why didn't they get it right the first time?" Quite the opposite, I am appreciative of Apple's commitment to their product and my role as a customer that they keep working on improvements. So, it is with this book. It is written as an upgrade to add a perspective for the many ideologies and methodologies already available. This book is not to question whether others "got it right the first time." Apple does not demand that I upgrade; it only makes it available. If I prefer my current version, I can dismiss the offer with a click of a button. Before you click the button to dismiss this offer, I ask only that you review its contents to see if an upgrade might serve your vision of leadership. Please keep in mind that upgrades typically require a system restart. The balance is that upgrades do not do away with prior content.

This book is a blend of my own perceptions sprinkled with a conglomerate of insights from published authors and experts. As an online adjunct faculty for two business colleges, I frequently remind my students that discussions should be a blend of knowledge, experience, and position supported by experts. Position alone is opinion. Knowledge alone is static. Experience as a solo act can be merely passion. It is the blend that engages potential. Experience can sometimes override formal education. One of my adult students became discouraged and told me, "I do not agree with the textbook." I told him that was marvelous and invited him to share his experience in the online discussion forum. Discussions are most lively when there is disagreement. Differences help us validate our commitment as well as opening our minds to incorporate other ideas. This book is a discussion prompt inviting an exchange of ideas. Prayerfully, by "the end" we can all be enriched from the dialogue.

Let's take a moment to talk about how God talks to us. Some believe that there is no audible voice while others profess that they hear God speaking. Some might believe that it is God speaking when the wind blows or a butterfly lands on their window. Others put their confidence only in the written scriptures or other sacred writings. If we consider the scriptures, then we accept that for Moses, God used a burning bush and His voice to speak (Exodus 3:2-4). For others, God used a dream or an event in nature and, in one infamous case, He used a donkey to speak (Numbers 22:28). What we can agree on is that there is a continuum of communication, and what is notable is that God knows how each of us learns. He communicates with us in ways that we understand. When you hear my expressions of *the Lord said* or *I heard God say*, it means an internal sense of a voice that has usually been accompanied by a pictorial prompt of some sort, e.g. a dream or a mental visualization. That is my disclaimer that I am not a heretic, blasphemer, or unstable (hopefully, you are smiling).

Many years ago, my children and I were living in a housing complex in Indianapolis, IN. In the middle of the night, I instantly awoke and heard, "You shall not die but live." I started praying and asking God what it meant (Psalm 118:17). A few minutes later, I heard my second son screaming, "Mom, they shot me." I jumped out of bed and ran to the top of the steps to see my 19-year old son crawling up the steps and leaving a trail of blood behind him. I pulled him to the top of the steps while believing that the shooters were inside of our apartment. He was ripping his pants down to reveal multiple bullet holes across the top of his legs. Do you remember the church mother's admonition that above all, I learn how to pray and call on the name of Jesus? I put my hands over the bullet holes and started praying. My son was screaming that he did not want to die, and the scripture that had awakened me became the banner over the situation. In my spirit, I heard, "I will bless the Lord at all times, and His praise will continually be in my mouth." I strongly advocate that every believer has a scripture that becomes their anthem verse. While there is obviously much more to this story, my son was transported to the hospital. The doctors told me that they would likely have to amputate both of his legs. I am also an advocate that your spiritual anthem should come with both verses and a chorus. The chorus of my anthem is to blurt out, "We will see what the Lord says." My son walked out of that hospital 36 hours later with both legs that the doctors said would need amputation. He walked out on crutches. He walked out wobbly, but he walked out.

One of the strongest encouragements you will hear from me is to look for the good and believe in miracles. God has a way of showing up and showing out when we least expect it. May I offer a little more detail about the night of that shooting? For some weeks, prior to that night, I had tried to get another phone line put into our apartment. On the day before the night of the shooting, the phone company finally came to install the second line. Earlier that evening, I had started walking toward the kitchen to check the safety bar on the patio door, but "something" in me told me to not to worry. I walked away. As my son was crawling up the steps, screaming, I had grabbed the phone from my room and the line was dead. The Spirit of the Lord told me not to worry. As I held my son who had been shot, his brother came out of the back bedroom upstairs and immediately started screaming that he was going to "get whoever did this." I told him to shut up, go back in his room and call for help. When he came back out, I said, "YOU are going to do nothing. You let God take care of this. How many more mothers have to go to an emergency room or a funeral before someone says stop. I told you to live for justice (explained later in the book)." We found out later that my son had been shot two blocks away. Because he had been shot in his upper legs, he crawled home. He started to hide behind the bushes in the front yard but could hear the shooters looking for him. He crawled to the back and found the open patio door. He tried to use the phone in the kitchen but pulled it and broke the cord (dead phone line). That is when he crawled up the stairs screaming. God had already put pieces of his miracle in place. Let's go back to the point of him leaving the hospital on crutches and find ourselves in the story.

Sometimes, we walk wobbly, but our focus needs to be on the fact that we are walking. When it seems that something in our life is so damaged that it becomes subject to amputation, we must have a resolve deep in our spirit that defies natural logic and even scholarly information. There must be a spiritual locus of control that takes charge and speaks loudly up over the voices of those who would say, "There is no hope." In fact, my son was not the target of the shooting. He happened to be in a house where the shooters were targeting another young man, and my son was in the way. Sometimes our life gets in the line of fire for something that was intended for someone else. The damage is real. The recovery time is necessary, but we can hold our head up and know, "I shall not die, but live, and declare the works of the LORD" (Psalm 118:17). By looking at the seven dimensions, we will find a path to recovery and boldness against prognosis that says we are not going to make it in one piece. Oh, yes we can, and yes, we will.

Chapter 1

Setting the Seven Dimensions

The presentation of seven dimensions of leadership is based on an inspiration the Lord shared with me several years ago. The initial application was to consider seven levels of human relationship, and I have used that model in ministry several times. You will find insights from that usage throughout this writing. Dreams are one way that God has opened my understanding or helped me to foresee a situation. It has been my custom to always ask, "Lord, where is that in the scripture?" The story of a message or a dream may not be in the Word, but there are applicable principles from the Bible. Having that practice has helped to maintain spiritual balance and proper interpretation long before I ever heard or understood words like hermeneutics, exegesis, or pericope. Opportunity to add education to experience has been a life bonus. What I am bringing is a blend of inspiration, experience, and education in a platform of exploring dimensions of leadership. More than examining leadership, my intention is to allow leaders a venue for self-examination. It is when we see ourselves clearly that we can see others and, most importantly, comprehend the course God is setting for us. Encouraging you to know yourself is one of the top priorities of this project.

I am a great believer in a sense of humor. In fact, it is my personal belief that those who laugh with you are the ones you can trust the most. Anyone can hand a tissue to me if I am crying, but when you understand my sense of humor and still love me, then surely, we are friends. It may not seem that the Bible is a book with a sense of humor, but I beg to differ. I confess that I had a hard time keeping a straight face with Job's opening discourse about why he did not deserve all the tragedy that came his way. Job asks in 6:8, ". . . is there any taste in the white of an egg?" All I can say is that I am grateful that I was not sitting in front of him when he posed that question as I could not have held my composure. Have you ever laughed at the wrong time, and the more you knew it was wrong, the funnier it all seemed? "Humor is created by surprising endings, unexpected events, people doing foolish things, incongruities between what people appear to be and really are, crafty motives, misidentifications, misunderstandings—all the stuff of human life, and all of it is in the Bible."[i] Perhaps our journey to the seventh dimension of leadership will allow you to pause and smile at some of your travels. Let us begin.

Foundation of the Message

For purposes of this book, we will consider the Samaritan woman as recorded in the Gospel of John 4:6-42 (RSV). The setting of the scene is that Jesus and his disciples had recently ministered in Judea and were traveling to Galilee. The Bible states that it was necessary for Him to travel through Samaria. It was not necessary for the sense of a travel requirement; rather, it was spiritually essential. He was weary from the travel and sat down at a well which is the location of His encounter with the woman we only know as "the woman at the well." The disciples have gone to get food, so the crowd has been reduced to a duo. During the conversation, Jesus asks the woman to go and get her husband. She answers, "I have no husband" (John 4:17a). Jesus responds to her with a truth that she undoubtedly could not have expected, "You are right in saying, 'I have no husband'; for you have had five husbands, and he whom you now have is not your husband; this you said truly" (John 4:17b-18). That interaction is the foundation for this book. The woman had seven relationships that are associated with our exploration, including five husbands, a live-in man, and Jesus Christ. The application of her scenario is not limited to male-female relationship dynamics. It serves as the leitmotiv for the stages of experience. The woman at the well is our teacher and our guide.

Before we go further, please allow me to hold a brief sidebar with you. This book is presented through the lens of biblical principles, but it is not written exclusively to Christians. For several years, it has been my privilege to serve as a chaplain in a men's correctional facility. My responsibility is not to be a Christian chaplain. I am a chaplain who happens to be a Christian. My role is to provide an opportunity for every religion that the Department of Corrections designates as a valid group, including Buddhist, Muslim, Wicca, Asatru, MSTA, Christians, Catholics, Jews, Hebrew Israelites, and others. My life is forever enriched by the opportunities to sit down and dialogue with men from each of the faiths as well as those who have no affiliation with an established religious group. The challenges of chaplaincy have repeatedly and consistently refined the way that I think and absolutely the way that I speak. We do not converse with the intention of proving one another right or wrong. Our conversations center around sharing perspectives with no persuasion attached. What we may find is that we are much more alike than we ever anticipated, and our differences are sometimes only semantics. In my interactions, I have not made a single observation that prompted me to question my faith. The diversity has encouraged me to be more committed to my own faith.

As one small example, the Bible has multiple references to the four winds, including the end-time gathering of people from the four winds (Matthew 24:31 and Mark 13:27). For many years, I participated in a 6:00 am prayer circle on Sunday morning. We prayed about that day's service, and the prayer always included the group turning to each of the four directions praying specific prayers for the four areas of our city. Imagine my surprise to discover that the Asatru (a pagan group based in Nordic culture) have a ritual that involves turning to the four directions and includes their god Thor. Imagine my surprise when I first witnessed the Wiccans (a pagan group) standing and calling souls from the north, south, east, and west. "The number of the basic spiritual personality types, by Hindu count, is four. Some people are primarily reflective. Others are basically emotional. Still others are essentially active. Finally, some are experimentally inclined."[ii] Hinduism and Buddhism customs use the four directions to establish completeness. "When the Lakota people pray or do anything sacred, they see the world as having four directions. From these four directions come the four winds. Each direction has a special meaning and color associated with it. The cross symbolizes all directions."[iii] The point to be made is that Christianity cannot operate in exclusivity. Far more diplomacy is accomplished with identifying similarities.

My interactions include a 3rd generation Satanist who, as a child, was baptized in the blood and urine of a prostitute according to his rituals. They include a conversation with a man whose entire face is tattooed to resemble Satan, including the horns. The Spirit of the Lord kept nudging me to ask if I could pray for him and his family. Proselytizing is forbidden in a prison, so I told him I had a question and let him know that he was welcome to decline. When I asked if I could pray for him, he said yes and then sat with tears running down his face as I prayed. Even with the affirmative response, I take the time to ask, "In my personal practice, I am a Christian. Is it all right with you if I pray according to my faith?" Questions empower people to share in an interaction versus taking the role of imposing beliefs. When the prayer was finished, the man said, "Chaplain, thank you for not judging me. This (pointing to his face) is something I did when I was a kid, and it does not speak to who I am today. Thank you for seeing beyond the appearance." The years in jail and prison ministry taught me to operate through the love that Jesus stated is both the first and great commandment and the second commandment of loving our neighbor. We love others based simply on the virtue of love. We do not create plans for other people. The truth is that most of the time when we want other people to change, it is to get them to fit our mold of what is right rather than allowing God to work in His timing. Love with no agenda is a skill that takes discipline to acquire and commitment to keep. This book is offered on a "love with no agenda" foundation.

During my years of interacting with our inmate Jewish population, I found many of them to be quite difficult. Their attitude typically came across as condescending and filled with entitlement. I strive for excellence, and it seemed that the Chapel was always coming up short for this group. One of the men said to me, "Chaplain Williams, we appreciate all of your efforts, but you will never get it right because you are not Jewish." No insult was intended, and no insult was taken. I understood his message. One day during their service, I heard an insight that completely altered my perspective. As the men were sharing about being the seed of Abraham, the lightbulb went on for me. What I perceived as entitlement was just that, but it was based on understanding their relationship to Yahweh. As sons, they felt authorized to certain rights as well as privileges. I do not knock on the door at my parents' home. I open the door and let myself in because I am their daughter and am entitled to be in their home. I do not have to ask permission to get in their refrigerator or sit in a chair. Our relationship is established in a way that allows me to have those liberties. How much stronger our faith would be as Christians if we grasped that concept. Paul teaches the Galatians that as believers, they have become the seed of Abraham (Galatians 3:7). "Let us, therefore, come boldly unto the throne of grace, that we may obtain mercy, and find grace to help in time of need" (Hebrews 4:16). We have an established relationship with God that allows us to be recipients of our connection.

Keep the woman at the well in your thoughts, and let's tie in the second significant piece of dispensations. The history of humanity, as we know it from the biblical record, can be divided into seven dispensations or periods of time. Dispensations represent various administrations of God to humanity. "Each one of these dispensations is said to represent a different way in which God deals with man, specifically a different testing for man."[iv] Each one has a distinguishing opening episode and a distinctive closing incident. The various dispensations have certain stewards and explicit responsibilities. This is a simplified table of the seven, but it will allow you to view the overall characteristics of each:

Figure 1.0. Dispensation Time Periods and Events

	DISPENSATION	BEGINNING	ENDING
1	Innocence	Creation	Expulsion from Eden
2	Conscience	Post-expulsion	Flood (Noah)
3	Authority	Post-flood	Tower of Babel
4	Promise	Post-Babel	Israel's bondage in Egypt
5	Law	Israel's bondage in Egypt	Crucifixion of Jesus Christ
6	Grace	Crucifixion of Jesus Christ	Present day
7	Sovereign Reign	Jesus' return to the earth	"Amen" of Book of Revelation

Source: Williams, 2016

It is thought-provoking that only the seventh dispensation is referred to as a reign, when, in fact, each of the other six periods of time is descriptive of the nature of God reigning and mankind's Plan B to that reign. This is where non-Christian believers may still benefit from the discussion as those periods of reign are what may be placed under the general concept of the kingdom of God.

With a secular view, it is "... a euphemism for social progress and political liberalization."[v] Secular is not intended as a term that implies less-than-spiritual but merely a view other than a Christian believer. In this case, secular broadens the scope of the conversation for those who would consider the Bible a book of history, philosophy or ideology. It is equally important to view the kingdom of God in more than spiritual terms. To do so would eliminate the historical perspective of its progression in the earth. There is a definite historical path that engages many disciplines, e.g. archeology, sociology, and anthropology. Perhaps most importantly, the collective application of the various disciplines gives us permission to frame a seven-dimension model of leadership that is presented here for your consideration.

As a visual learner, I often interpret what is said through mental pictures. On an overhead projector, it is possible to lay a transparency with data or images and then lay another one on top of the first one to add more detail. To arrive where we are striving to go in this book, consider the parallels of the Samaritan woman to the dispensations.

Figure 1.1. Dispensations and Relationships

	DISPENSATION	RELATIONSHIP
1	Innocence	Husband #1
2	Conscience	Husband #2
3	Authority	Husband #3
4	Promise	Husband #4
5	Law	Husband #5
6	Grace	Live-in relationship
7	Sovereign Reign	Jesus Christ

Source: Williams, 2016

With each dispensation, there are strengths and weaknesses relative to the characteristic of a specific age. As a quick example, the strength of innocence is that there is no prior history; therefore, there are no preconceived ideas about what will or will not take place. That leaves innocence free of bias, prejudice, and other modes of thinking that favor one person over another. The weakness of that same innocence is naiveté which leaves vulnerabilities in place and opportunities for others (like the serpent) to take advantage of the person. Naiveté becomes the prey of the hunter. Have you ever had someone blurt out the ending of a movie? It ruins the pleasure of watching the story unfold! With that in mind, we will not go any deeper into the example as it would become a spoiler for the script.

Of the many men that I have ministered to, several have been victims of sexual abuse in their childhood. Here is an approach that has proven useful in helping them. Indiana is a state that is supposed to experience snow and ice in the winter months. A few years ago, the temperature was nearly 70 degrees in December. While that is an unseasonable temperature, it did not cause it to not be winter. Children are not meant to be sexual. It is an unseasonable action. That does not make them not be children. It is a horrible mixed message for a child to perform sexual acts while also learning to spell their name or color in the lines. Children are not supposed to know how to perform oral sex and then jump rope or play kickball during recess. It is not just sexual activity but other traumatic events. *Brief Sidebar: Please know that in no way do I believe that having been victimized removes the responsibility of accountability. Being a victim is not an excuse for becoming an offender. It is a whole other discussion for me to express the systemic changes that I favor for bringing both correction and healing to men who have been victimized, and subsequently, became offenders.*

One man who was nearly 70 years old sat in my office and told me that as a young boy, he had watched his dad shoot his mom with a rifle. Because of her death and his dad's arrest, the boy was sent to live with an uncle and his wife. Those adults proceeded to tell him, "No need to cry now. It's over." As he sat in my office with tears running down his face, he said it was the first time he had ever felt safe enough to weep about watching his mom die. When it does not snow in Indiana in the winter, the ground does not absorb the needed water to prepare for the growing season of spring. That is only one of numerous penalties from unseasonable patterns. What is unseasonable in one stage causes consequences in future stages. As we address the various dispensations, we will consider what is unseasonable and how those anomalies influence future phases.

Analysis Synopsis

There are two modes of study that are essential to correctly using both the woman at the well and the dispensations. The first is taken from Duvall and Hayes (2012) and their five-step process for transitioning from the ancient world of biblical culture to modern society. Here is a graph of that process:

Figure 1.2. Five-Step Process for Grasping Scripture

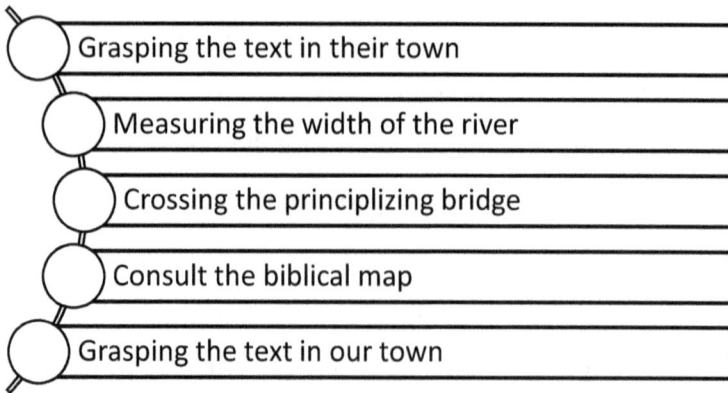

Step	
○	Grasping the text in their town
○	Measuring the width of the river
○	Crossing the principlizing bridge
○	Consult the biblical map
○	Grasping the text in our town

Source: Duvall & Hays, 2012

As the authors point out, "We are separated from the biblical audience by culture and customs, language, situation, and a vast expanse of time."[vi] No more than the average 21st-century citizen can grasp pioneering with covered wagons or using squirrel guns to fight a war can we accurately grasp a woman who goes to a well daily to draw water or the walking ministry of Jesus and his disciples. What we can do is use the woman's encounter as a pattern to address issues that are still flourishing despite over 2,000 years of human advancement. "Just as Jesus cut through deep prejudices of race, religion, gender, and class to make meaningful contact with the Samaritan woman, so [...today bear witness to] how Christ meets them directly in their various contexts."[vii] If necessary to make this conversation compatible to your beliefs, consider Christ as a historical or literary figure.

Even as the dimensions are progressive, so the context encompasses generations and historical settings. What begins in Eden concludes with the willingness of modern leaders to grasp their journey in its intricacies. The socio-rhetorical analysis will serve as the compass for this journey to ensure that we are accurate not only in the overall direction but in the description of the setting. For those not familiar with the term, let us hold another brief sidebar using Robbins (1996),

> "The hyphenated prefix *socio-* refers to the rich resources of modern anthropology and sociology that socio-rhetorical criticism brings to the interpretation of a text. The term *rhetorical* refers to the way language in a text is a means of communication among people."[viii]

There are five subsets within this mode of analysis. Those include inner texture, intertexture, social and cultural texture, ideological texture, and sacred texture. In its simplest definition, "Inner texture analysis focuses on words as tools for communication."[ix] In more detail, inner texture means getting inside of the communication and examining patterns of words, voices that are speaking, and other devices that give meaning to the text. "Intertexture is a text's representation of, reference to, and use of phenomena in the 'world' outside the text being interpreted."[x] In other words, it establishes compatibility to the world in which the text is written. The social and cultural texture is self-explanatory and one of my favorite modes of analysis. The ideological texture is my preference due to its focus on people. ". . . ideological texture concerns the biases, opinions, preferences, and stereotypes of a particular writer and a particular reader."[xi] Finally, the sacred texture is a search for the divine through the voice of the text. How is God speaking? What is God saying? How is God present?

Personalizing the Context

It may seem that there is an excessive amount of attention to setting the context of our search in the seven dimensions of leadership; however, it is an intentional framing that will be beneficial throughout the reading. Have you ever been in a conversation when you eventually realized that there were two entirely different conversations taking place? Effective communication is becoming more and more an art form, particularly in our multi-generational workforce and our dependency on technological-based communication versus face-to-face conversations. As a chaplain in a men's prison, it is my responsibility to ask for ID's and compare them to a check-off list to allow inmates into various services. It is my intention to be polite and to be cheerful. One evening as I checked in various individuals, I said, "Have a good evening, sir" to which the person stopped and said, "I am NOT a sir." I had a choice to create a conflict with the individual or to pursue peace. Solomon said in Ecclesiastes 9:18 that wisdom is better than conflict. During the service, I walked over to the individual and apologized for the misunderstanding. He pleasantly said that he was not offended and knew that I meant no harm. After that, I worked even harder on being aware and sensitive and consciously eliminated pronouns from my vocabulary. The increasing presence of the LGBTQ (Lesbian Gay Bisexual Transgender Questioning) community should set a demand on all of us to heighten our mindfulness and understanding. That is but one small example of setting a framework for communication to ensure both parties are in the same conversation.

Each of us brings our history with us to every interaction. Have you ever had someone that you simply did not like? You could not pinpoint exactly what about that person became a trigger for your distaste, but it was there. We can explore this from empirical research. "A balanced state occurs when triadic relations among an individual (p), another person (o), and an attitude object (x) are harmonious. Balance occurs when all three relations among p, o, and x are positive, or when one relation is positive and two are negative. When the triad is imbalanced, tension exists."[xii] Social psychologists attribute our likes and dislikes to a process called *cognitive evaluation*. In amateur terms, we evaluate others based on our history. Jesus was clearly masterful at not giving way to that mode of thinking. Otherwise, none of us could have become recipients of his ministry. Just as clearly, his disciples needed more development in this area as John records their reaction, "Just then his disciples came. They marveled that he was talking with a woman . . ." (John 4:27, RSV). Samaritans had a lineage of Jewish and pagan tribes mixing which made them hated by other Jews. "Rather than contaminate themselves by passing through Samaritan territory, Jews who were traveling from Judea to Galilee or vice versa would cross over the river Jordan, bypass Samaria by going through Transjordan, and cross over the river again as they neared their destination."[xiii] Jesus was undoubtedly "on the wrong side of the tracks" when he chose to go through Samaria. As we walk through the dimensions of leadership, we will closely examine how destiny finds us despite societal, racial, or cultural differences.

For the Christian believers who will read this book, be prepared to have traditions and rituals challenged. There is a revolutionary undergirding to this writing. We are not coming together throughout these pages to perpetuate cycles but to engage in self-examination that just might turn our world upside down. The beauty of the outcome is that the world undeniably is not flat, and you have the assurance that you will not fall off into oblivion. For those other than Christians who will read this book, criticizing Christianity is not the objective. Through the lens of your own faith practices, you will also be invited to a journey of examination that just possibly will inspire you to let go of the mundane and embrace radical thinking. Perhaps readers will need a box of tissue for their tears, an icepack for the bruises, and a Band-Aid or two; however, the joy and achievement of crossing the finish line will be worth any discomforts of the journey. "Everything you will ever do as a leader is based on one audacious assumption. It's the assumption that you matter."[xiv] That assumption is our guiding force. One other essential piece to setting the tone for this book is to remind the readers that while there is a reasonable progression of the seven dimensions, there are times in life where there may be an overlap or a repeat of various dimensions. This is not a step-by-step guide to becoming the perfect leader. First, there is no such person. Second, as my spiritual mentor Genevieve DeBow used to say, "None of us have arrived because the minute you think you did, you didn't."[xv]

Life has taught me that sometimes God uses our heart (our passion) to draw us out of one situation and into another so that He can then show us, "This is what I really want you to do." When we are passionate, we embrace accountability. "The result of this is people become impassioned about their role in the company's welfare and their own professional development -- something that is actually quite personal and close to the heart. This newfound passion is the driver for productivity."[xvi] When Jesus encounters the woman at the well, we see the flame of her passion for worship move from a stage of smoldering to burning so brightly that the greater part of a city is converted. Our central character, the woman at the well, will illustrate the overlap and ultimately, the clarity for the destiny that comes with entering the seventh dimension of sovereign reign. As she progresses through innocence, conscience, authority, promise, law, grace, and sovereign reign, we will not become judges and critics but participants in her story. More specifically, her story will become our story.   Where do we begin? As Glinda said to Dorothy in the 1939 *Wizard of Oz,* "It's always best that you start at the beginning . . .."[xvii]

Reading Between the Lines

A significant struggle in writing this book is finding the point of blending knowledge and testimony. In the back of my mind, I heard the voice of a pastor that told me I probably did not have a call to ministry. My gift was talking, and that was different than men who were called to preach. I recalled the sting of being part of a ministry that said women are too emotional to be trusted with ministry. May I confess that I was moving along at a blazing speed in my doctoral journey until I started writing this book? I got to what I thought was the end of the first chapter and froze. I stayed frozen for over a month. I started checking myself for signs of depression. No, that was not the problem. In my head, the clock was ticking, and I knew that my deadline for draft completion was getting further and further away. I negotiated with myself and said, "What difference does it make if you take an extra semester to completion?" In Romans 7:13-25, Paul writes about the internal conflict that we all experience. He admits that he gives in

to what he knows is wrong, and he avoids what he knows is right.
If I were writing an exegetical analysis, my grade might be zero for
the application of Paul's words. On the other hand, if I use
ideological texture, then his words mean what I need for them to
mean through the lens of my understanding. The greatest
application of his words is for me to admit my struggle in writing
and find the voice that speaks to my story while not discounting the
intellectual.

The reason I can write on behalf of the woman at the well
is that she and I could have exchanged places in history. Perhaps
my weeks of feeling frozen was an internal struggle with just how
much to share and to be sure that what I share has purpose. I had
a string of relationships before my ultimate encounter with Jesus
as Sovereign. My interracial relationship in 1971 was a societal
faux pau but exceptionally so in a small Midwestern town.
Miscegenation had only been legalized a few years prior. My
transition from Caucasian Catholic school girl to drug-addicted
high school dropout was swift, but the seed of that explosion had
been planted years earlier in the breaking of innocence. You are
the only one who knows the timing of your breaking away from
innocence, or perhaps you are not able to identify any details at
all. Either way, all of us have a point in our lives where we

recognize that our innocence is behind us. Where you went when you took the next step is what deserves attention.

Finally, I realized that the key to finding expression for the woman at the well in this book is for me to use the voice of my story. Maybe it is your story, too (or a similar version). Sometimes the mere recognition of having a story is a breakthrough. Perhaps what the world needs is not just one more book about leadership but one in which the reader can find him- or herself between the lines and finally be free of the cycle of repeating dimensions. Sometimes opportunity comes right up to the door and then steps away before we can invite it to have a seat. That does not mean the knock won't come again.

At one point during my studies at IUPUI, the Vice-Chancellor of Undergraduate Education told me that he loved the way I write. He asked if I could take some of my writing to share with a friend of his. He said the two of them took a fishing trip on the Mississippi River each year. I was appreciative of his feedback and agreed to let him take a collection of my writing. He apologetically gave the work back to me several weeks later and told me that his fishing buddy had died suddenly of a massive heart attack. He had not previously told me that his friend was Alex Haley, the author of <u>Roots</u>. Losing that one opportunity did not mean that no more opportunities would come. Solomon tells us that, "To every thing there is a season, and a time to every purpose under the heaven" (Ecclesiastes 3:1). As we walk through the first six dispensations, remember that there is a season and a time assigned to your destiny. Together, let's step toward the seventh dimension and walk in the freedom of sovereign reign.

Chapter 2

First Dimension of Innocence

All of us have experienced this stage of life. For some, it lasted only during childhood. For others, it did not transition until sometime in adolescence or adulthood. It may have been as we found our first love. It may have been believing that we could be President of the United States (lofty vision for a girl born in 1954), becoming famous or wealthy, or conquering Mt. Everest. Innocence is what allowed us to believe in Santa Claus, the Easter Bunny, and the Tooth Fairy. Innocence has an untainted ability to be a dreamer. In maturity, we must be cautious that innocence does not become a rejection of reality. In leadership, innocence may have believed that you could change the world. Maybe not quite so lofty, but perhaps your innocence inspired you to believe that having a vision statement meant everyone in the company would work toward that end. The goal for discussing innocence is to balance the principle of it with utility. A 1966 article by M.J. Rossant cites the Eisenhower Administration as naïve and equating innocence to false security. One of the descriptions of President Eisenhower's time in office is that it became "a holiday from history." The absence of history, however, can be disorienting, and, as Rossant points out, it can become a point of false security.

One of the many intense moments of being a chaplain came during a time of using the woman at the well and the seven dispensations in a message. As the inmates and I explored the breaking of innocence, one of the men shared the following story followed by a question that is still stirring in me. He said that his earliest memory (around the age of 2) of his dad involved his dad on top of his mom beating her. After that, he was taken to another state to live with his grandma who had custody of other cousins. When grandma would go out of the house, an older cousin would take the little boy's hand and use it to fondle herself. If she spotted grandma coming back, she shoved the boy's hand away and made it clear that he was not supposed to tell. In retrospect, he understood that his exposure to sexual activity was bundled with deceit, lying, and secret keeping. There is more to his story, but with tears running down his face, he asked: "What do you do when your innocence is taken before you know what innocence is?" As leaders, we wish that the title came bundled with having the right answers at the right time. With tears running down my face, I could only affirm the depths of his question and say, "Sometimes phrasing the question is the beginning of finding the answer."

How many times in life have we not only not known the answer, but we could not even find a way to word the question?

The Value of Question

Life has taught me that the Bible is not a book of answers, but a book filled with questions. Here is an abbreviated list of some of my favorite questions from the scripture:

Figure 2.0. Scripture Citations and Biblical Questions

SCRIPTURE	QUESTION
Genesis 18:14	Is there any thing too hard for the Lord?
Exodus 4:2	What is that in your hand?
Jeremiah 8:22	Is there no balm in Gilead; is there no physician there? why then is not the health of the daughter of my people recovered?
Matthew 16:15	Who do you say that I am?
Romans 8:31	If God is for us, who can be against us?
Romans 8:35	Who shall separate us from the love of Christ?

Source: Williams, 2016

The inclusion of questions has value to our discussion because questions are not always an interrogative tool for arriving at a conclusion but an invitation to deeper relationship. Particularly when God is asking the question, He does not do so out of a need for information or clarification. In a counseling session with a young inmate, he was amazed when I suggested to him that his wife did not ask questions expecting to hear yes or no responses. I said, "For instance if she asks if you like her outfit, she is not waiting on you to respond with *yes*. She is inviting you into the relationship and wants to hear, "Oh, yes, you look beautiful, and the color of your eyes make the whole outfit talk to me!" After a few more examples, he said, "I never thought of that! I am going to use that on our next visit!" There are times that circumstances are frustrating or perhaps even totally defeating, but if we will turn to relationship and be open to questions, there is a depth that takes us to a place described by Philippians 4:7, "And the peace of God, which passes all understanding . . . ." A positive relationship is not merely the product of correctly worded questions but of insightful responses that further the interaction.

"It is not possible to become a good thinker and be a poor questioner."[xviii] Intellectuals are not determined by answers but by questions. Fresh questions are what keeps thinking lively and continues to stir the potential in individuals, ultimately radiating outwardly to culture and society. "The questions we ask can tell us as much about ourselves as they do about the subject, person, or issue we are questioning."[xix] We find evidence in this from the Genesis account where the serpent's descriptor is that he is subtle. His description precedes the question he poses. Paul and Elder (2006) generated a chart describing the following three categories of questions:

Figure 2.1. Categories of Questions

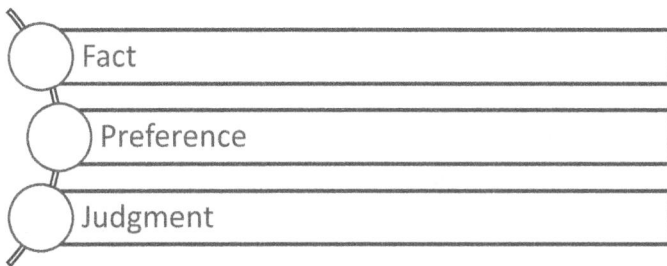

Source: Paul & Elder, 2006

Questions of fact will typically have a right or wrong response. Preference has multiple options, e.g., favorite color. Judgment engages reasoning and must go beyond fact or preference. It is the type of reasoning that determines authentic critical thinking. "Any question calls on us to do one of three things: (1) to express a subjective preference, (2) to establish an objective fact, or (3) to come up with the best of competing answers."[xx] A principal learning experience for leaders is to master questioning. If nothing else, single parenting taught me well not to answer questions with responses but to respond with a question. Most of the time, the person asking the question knows the answer but does not want the responsibility for the outcome. If they ask me, and I answer, then the outcome somehow becomes my fault. Jesus was a master of questions. Luke 20:20-26 tells a story of men who came to Jesus asking him about whether they should pay taxes. "Show me a coin. Whose likeness and inscription has it?" They said, "Caesar's" (Luke 20:24).

Through the role God had assigned to Adam and Eve to exercise dominion, Eve was in a leadership position; however, Eve's innocence had no means to frame reciprocal questions for the serpent. Whenever a conversation has only one side capable of asking questions, it leaves a distinct advantage to that person. One-sided questioning is an interrogation. The serpent's inquisition became his vantage point to plant seeds of doubt. Innocence holds confidence that all parties have a righteous agenda. If we look at Eve through the lens of criminogenic performance, we find behavioral evidence that she was innocent. "Innocent suspects often behave in predictable ways in investigative contexts. They plan their verbal behavior less and are less likely to utilize a specific strategy in order to be believed."[xxi] Eve had no basis to consider that the dialogue with the serpent was anything less than a conversation. Innocence believes in a just world. Innocence believes there is no need of queries. The presence of questions that cannot be quickly answered becomes interpreted as a gap in the relationship. Using that as a Segway, let us consider the model of learning organizations and the valuing of questions.

"The core of learning organization work is based on five learning disciplines – lifelong programs of study and practice:"[xxii] Those five disciplines are:

Figure 2.2. Disciplines in Learning Organizations

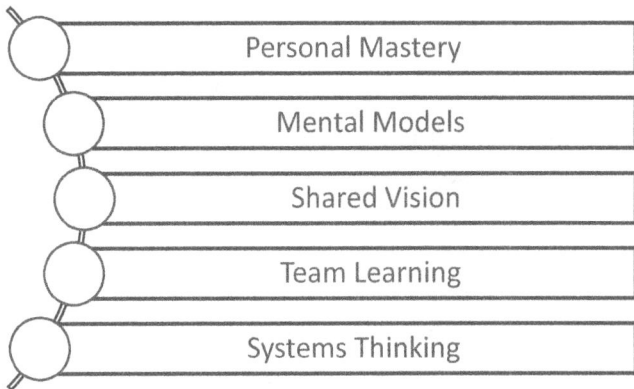

- Personal Mastery
- Mental Models
- Shared Vision
- Team Learning
- Systems Thinking

Source: Senge, Kleiner, Roberts, Ross, & Smith, 1994

Adam and Eve were given an opportunity for personal mastery from the moment of their creation. The naming of the animals and the stewardship of the garden became their learning laboratory. Personal mastery provides means for each person to develop in goals that they set. The mental model references how we see the world which forms our thought processes and subsequent actions. In the case of the historic Eden, the daily walks with God are likely the point of contact that reached into a shared vision. Team learning blends the individual's growth into the collective energy of the group. This is the point of synergy. Systems thinking is the desired outcome, ". . . a way of thinking about, and a language for describing and understanding, the forces and interrelationships that shape the behavior of systems."[xxiii] This is the point that the serpent infected the original plan God had for mankind. His persuasion of Eve to consider that questions implied a gap in how she was valued or the credibility of her role in the bigger picture caused a breakdown in systems thinking.

Learning organizations are not destroyed by failure or setbacks. They, in fact, thrive by valuing failure as an opportunity to grow. That is what God did when he imposed explicit consequences to Adam and Eve. Each of them became part of a systemically repairing shift. For Adam, production would come with more exertion, but it endured as an opportunity. For Eve, multiplication of humanity became her systemic contribution, albeit that it would come through an increased struggle. The outcome from their expulsion is a perfect fit to the core concept of a learning organization, "Learning in organizations means the continuous testing of experience, and the transformation of that experience into knowledge – accessible to the whole organization, and relative to its core purpose."[xxiv] Whereas God's original blueprint for creation set in seasons, the outcome of mankind's fall included the principles of cycles. The cyclical nature of working for productivity and the birthing process reinforced the nonlinear origins of our world. In each case, there was not a new activity introduced to either one. What they were already doing now came partnered with greater intensity.

Linear vs. Circular Reasoning

Innocence is based on linear thinking. Point A leads to Point B and so on. Step 1 is followed by Step 2 and so on. There is no room for optional considerations. Most of us use linear thinking in groundwork activities, e.g. the way we get dressed for work, the methods we have for preparing a meal. It is not that linear thinking must be removed from our range of processing.

"The thinking style of people in Western society is greatly influenced by a worldview grounded in the Newtonian reductionist, determinist, and equilibrium-oriented tradition in which any system is composed of divisible parts."[xxv] This thinking operates in the belief that if the parts can be understood, then the whole can be understood. "Nonlinear dynamical systems are highly complex and often rapidly changing, where a multitude of interrelated and interdependent parts contribute to outcomes that are very difficult to predict."[xxvi] Nonlinear thinking values instinct as much as experience and experience as much as knowledge. As a brief pitch for Human Resource professionals, it is their role to consider the use of the Myers-Briggs Type Indicator (MBTI) as part of the interviewing of candidates. Measuring personality types is an essential element to talent management in the 21st century. Consider this distinction,

Figure 2.3. Linear and Nonlinear Thinking

LINEAR THINKING	NONLINEAR THINKING
Preference for attending to external data and facts and processing this information through conscious logic and rational thinking to form knowledge, understanding, or a	*Preference for attending to internal feelings, impressions, and sensations; and processing this information (both consciously and subconsciously) to "intuit" or form knowledge,*

decision for guiding subsequent action.	*understanding, or a decision for guiding subsequent action."*

Source: Vance, Groves, & Yongsun, 2004

Perhaps what Adam and Eve did not understand in their state of innocence is that failure is only failure when nothing new is learned. In other words, failure is simply a learning opportunity that opens the next door. Perhaps the expulsion was an extraction that unlocked innovative potential. It is our seemingly innate distaste for change that compelled the posting of the cherub with the flaming sword. Modern leaders might learn from our historic characters as we sometimes fight change and strive to cling to the familiar when we might benefit from a cherub with a flaming sword blocking our path of return. In our mistakes, we become liberated to learning; therefore, the circular nature of experience becomes its own best practice.

Eliminating Coincidence

Can you remember the first time you realized that you were a leader? It may have been choosing teams in a neighborhood kickball team or selection as captain of some project in school. Take a step forward in time and recall the first promotion in the workplace and the sense that, "This is going to be great!" Unfortunately, most of us confused our role of being the one in charge with leadership or having broader responsibilities with expanded influence. The truism is fitting, "If only I had known then what I know now." Innocence believes that promotions come because others see our potential and want what is best for us. Innocence does not pause to consider ulterior motives. Like Eve, it is usually only in the aftermath of having innocence violated that we recognize who is and who is not well-intended. If time and space permitted, we could use that consideration as an opening to an entire volume on workplace politics.

The violation of innocence is categorically associated with someone playing the role of the serpent. In the King James Version, the description is that the serpent is subtle, which is *aruwm* in Hebrew. The adjective *aruwm* describes someone who is crafty, prudent, sensible, and shrewd. It also means sly, but let's focus on the previous descriptors. Perhaps you are the one who is responsible for the breaking of innocence in others. Accountability and responsibility are separate concepts. Sometimes we remain unhealed because we function in the all or nothing mentality of "guilty or not guilty." Exploring the word *aruwm* gives us pause for thought that many times innocence is violated by legitimate relationships that have become unbalanced. Genesis 1:26-27 describes the creation of man (including both male and female) with a specific assignment that they should have dominion in the earth. It was their role to subjugate creation. In Genesis 3:1-8, we find the narrative of the serpent inspiring Eve to eat from the tree that was in the middle of the garden.

When innocence is violated, the outcome is disparity. Eve was assigned to a place of leadership, yet she gave ear to logic that provoked her to believe differently. The moment she listened to words that sparked doubt, she compromised her position of dominion and immediately became subject to the fall. None of us fall in one quick step. We first engage in a thought process that results in action. It can happen in a moment, or it may happen over time. Eve questioned the parameters of her destiny and participated with the voice of mutiny. It is strategic that the tree was in the middle of the garden. It was the fulcrum of creation between heaven and earth, between God and mankind. The sentence of death that God has spoken is not just a natural death but a breach in the pattern of life. From the moment that we negotiate our destiny to the voice of uncertainty, we have engaged the dynamic of captivity. Levels of bondage will be addressed in the dispensation of law.

Brief Interjection

*For those of you reading this book that are in ministry, there is a special message for you. If you sincerely believe that ministry is your calling in life, then it must **become** your life. You cannot give God a part of you. I have told many young ministers, "Understanding destiny means that your calling will cost you the next beat of your heart and the breath of your lungs." One thing I do know is that you will never resent destiny. Find a mentor and listen to their wisdom. Be completely honest and hold nothing back. We all need someone in our life who is safe and can hear what is going on inside of us. I greatly respect one of my mentors for allowing me, as a young woman, to see her humanity. She did not allow me to put her on a pedestal. We do not need untouchable people in our lives, nor do we need to become untouchable. There will always be temptations for you to lessen the intensity of your calling, but keep the flame on high! That does not mean that you do not have balance, but that is a skill that takes time to acquire. Be gracious to yourself. Give yourself space to learn. If you have an "Eve" moment and find yourself talking to a serpent, remember that innocence is but one stage. It is not the end of the story. Don't give up! One of my personal sayings is, "Whatever it is, God is more."*

For those who relate the breaking of innocence to a sexual act (consensual), it is not just a physiological experience. It has been proven to be a psychological experience. "When two people are intimate, the hypothalamus in the brain releases chemicals that induce feelings of attachment and trust. Having sex . . . results in a person forming an attachment and trusting someone with whom he or she does not have a committed relationship. The definition of trust in the mind deteriorates."[xxvii] The repeated breaking of trust carries over to our spiritual capacity in the ultimate relationship – trusting God. Jesus' interaction with the woman at the well was about trust much more than it was about a drink of water. "The Samaritan woman said to him, "How is it that you, a Jew, ask a drink of me, a woman of Samaria?" For Jews have no dealings with Samaritans" (John 4:9, RSV). The woman's response displays various psychological barriers to trust, including filtering, closed mind, and premature evaluation. Remember that Jesus merely made a request, "Give me a drink" (John 4:7). Instead of a *yes* or *no* response, the woman went into a negative response based on ethnicity and culture. "Lack of trust makes them derive negative meaning of the message . . .."[xxviii]

Let us consider another aspect of this story. If we believe that everything about Jesus' presence in the earth is supernaturally ordained, then we also accept that there are no coincidental occasions in His story. The disciples going away to find food is not a fluke but a prearrangement. When trust levels are exceptionally low, it is the quietness of an environment that can compel a person to focus on the situation at hand rather than depend on distraction as an avoidance mechanism. There was no one at the well but Jesus and the woman. Her quickness to become her own distraction with ideological texture questions is a robust signal of how deeply broken her trust levels had become. David DeSteno, Ph.D. (2014) notes a trust mechanism as, ". . . *forward-looking myopia* or our tendency to focus more on the present than on the future."[xxix] The breaking of innocence has the capacity to lock a person into behaviors and thinking patterns that are stuck in the present. Further, it results in a person battling the present with unresolved past hurts which can emotionally, mentally, spiritually, and even physically propel us (the woman) deeper into a mode of *spinning our wheels* where there is a lot of visible movement but no actual progress.

Let's make this specific to those in leadership roles. Kouzes and Posner (2011) propose a model of The Five Practices of Exemplary Leadership that include:

Figure 2.4. Five Practices of Exemplary Leadership

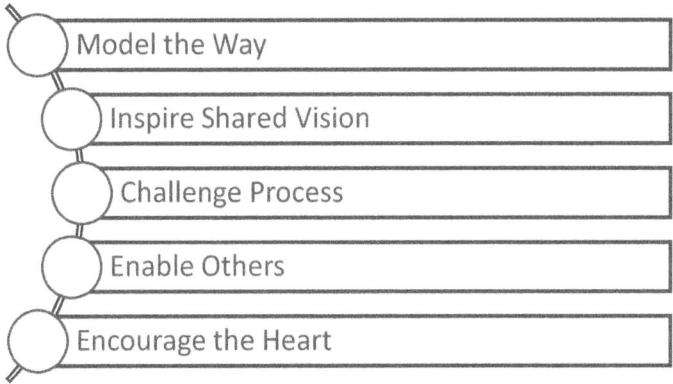

| Model the Way |
| Inspire Shared Vision |
| Challenge Process |
| Enable Others |
| Encourage the Heart |

Source: Kouzes & Posner, 2011

The authors state, "You must clarify values by finding your voice."[xxx] You owe it to yourself to find your truth. Many times, the label or title associated with a position becomes mistaken for the truth of a person's identity. If that has happened or is currently the situation in your leadership journey, it is not too late to find healing. If the first step of modeling the way is dependent on finding your voice, then step five of encouraging the heart of others necessitates your healing. For some, working their way into leadership has been their self-prescribed effort to counter the breaking of their innocence. In that scenario, making decisions and being in charge is the daily medication. These are the people who cannot relax away from the job (or ministry), who keep their cell phones on 24-7, or who refuse to take vacations on the premise of being "needed" at the office.

When my sons were in junior high, some of their classmates told them, "Your Mom is a n----- loving whore." They wanted to fight. They came home angry and ready to defend my honor. I told them to let it go. They thought I was crazy. I said, "No, you don't fight. You live for justice. Justice has nothing to do with getting even. Pure justice says when the power is in your hands, you do better than what was done to you. Live for justice." Some of you may have a late start on the mission for justice, but I encourage you to pick up the mantle and live by that mantra. Your mission is not to change or fix the ones who may be guilty of breaking your innocence. Your objective is to use your circumstance to live for justice. In 2 Corinthians 5:18, Paul instructs us to operate in a ministry of reconciliation. That means that we operate in exchange. Anything and everything we have experienced in life have value if we give it to the Lord. That teaching is an analogy for a currency exchange or exchange of value. If we surrender our earthly experiences to God, we gain kingdom currency in exchange. We trade hate for love, war for peace, anger for wisdom, and much more. We live in a time of revolutionary change. "Change has changed. No longer is it an additive. No longer does it move in a straight line. In the twenty-first century, change is discontinuous, abrupt, and seditious."[xxxi] We can learn from the dispensation of innocence and from our character, the woman at the well that change is essential to leaders stretching into the next phase of development. Our naiveté and its eventual release is merely the platform for our launching into opportunity.

To some degree, we can equate innocence with ignorance, meaning lack of knowledge and experience. While raising my children, I often explained my decisions to them in detail. In their opinion, it was too much. One of my sons told me once, "Mom, we don't really need to know all of that!" My response was this, "I am giving you information so that you will never make a thoughtless choice. You might make an ignorant choice, but you won't make a choice where you had no information." Innocence is protective and strives to eliminate all risks and threats to that. While the idea of living in a castle is the center of most fairy tales, the flip side of that is the same high walls that protect also block the scenery that surrounds the fortress. It would seem foreign to many modern families but for me and my siblings, playing outside was an expectation, even in the winter. My mother would say, "It is healthy for you. Go outside!" We might even consider the story of Job where God had Job behind a protective hedge. Satan's accusation could be paraphrased to say, "You don't let him have a blend of experiences." None of us would permit our children to only eat dessert. They may not want the vegetables, but the spinach is necessary. The change of address from Eden to the rest of the world opened the gateway for experience. It was God's way of saying, "Go outside and play. It is healthy for you."

In professional realms, a person being naïve is not a compliment. It infers a lack of experience. Advocating for creative thinking and innovation in contemporary leadership, Eden becomes the perfect laboratory.

"Nature doesn't care if patterns are creative or destructive. What matters to nature is the way things self-organize, the way they cooperate to form coherent patterns. When you look at nature's patterns, contents are contained anywhere but are revealed only in the dynamics."[xxxii]

The dilemma with a laboratory setting is that it does not equate to a holistic environment. It becomes locked into an experimental loop. To be completely operational, whatever is being tested must be put on the market. What is traditionally interpreted as a downfall in Eden becomes the springboard for humankind to leap from innocence to maturity. The breaking of innocence does indeed compel a new set of decision making.

> "We decide what makes us significant or insignificant. We decide to be creative or indifferent. We decide. We choose. In the end, our own creativity is decided by what we choose to do or what we refuse to do. And as we decide or choose, so are our destinies formed."[xxxiii]

When I was a child, spankings did not result in the child reporting the parent for abuse. If it was my mother, the spanking was likely with her hand or a fly swatter. If it was, "Wait until you father gets home," the spanking was going to include a belt. The physical correction was not intended to cause injury. It was an intervention that halted a behavior. When Adam and Eve violated the Eden environment, God interjected an intervention that halted their behavior. In His wisdom, consequences were imposed that unleashed innovation. Adam and Eve still had to engage with creation but now on a different set of terms. "Innovation . . . includes management of large amounts of creativity. Specifically, innovation requires processes, structures, and resources to manage significant levels of creativity."[xxxiv] In the moment, the punishment seemed severe, but God was actually equipping the couple for a creative revolution as He released them to a broader scope of responsibility.

Another layer that is extremely uncomfortable for most is to consider God's role in the existence of evil. If we trust that He is ultimately God of everything, then we accept that evil exists because He allows. To what end then can we use that as a force of growth? Genesis 3:22 states that God's concern for the couple is that they now *know* good and evil. Cautiously engaging the simplicity of a concordance meaning, the word *know* is *yada* which speaks to having an acquaintance with good and evil. Prior to eating the fruit, the presence of evil had nothing to do with their assignment to steward the earth or their relationship with God. Now that they have put themselves on an acquaintance level with evil as well as good, their decision-making processes had to upgrade (our Chapter 1 suggestion) to keep pace with the elements of their environment. Another aspect of the word *know* is to mean that they made themselves known to good and evil. Genesis 3:7 says that as soon as Adam and Eve ate of the fruit, their eyes were opened, and the first result is that they *knew (yada)* that they were naked. Is it that they were previously unaware? No, but now their awareness is two-dimensional rather than the singular lens of innocence.

Application

What is the message from innocence? In ministry with this message, we would reach into the first dimension of disappointment. It is ultimately how we handle disappointments and detours that develop character. In presenting a workshop or writing a consultant's report, this exploration allows recommendations and initiatives to challenge and support leadership growth programs. For one of my doctoral projects, I interviewed a person in a prominent government position. In our conversation, the person expressed a tendency to internally question their worth. This individual has been influential in facilitating numerous programs over a period of several decades. The conversation between the serpent and Eve merely exposed Eve's internal uncertainty about her worth to the administration of innocence. That uncertainty prompted her to act against her notion of potential rejection that was, in fact, an illusion created by the words of the serpent. The idea that God (administration) was holding out on allowing her to be equitable prompted Eve to re-negotiate the relationship. Executive coaching ensures that the Eve in each of us develops a Leadership Point of View (LPV). The LVP becomes a stabilizer. "Leaders must continually broaden their vision and deepen their insight . . .."[xxxv]

Whether in a one-to-one coaching relationship, facilitating a group program, or presenting a consultant's report, approaching the concept of innocence in leadership must be partnered with assessments and a plan of action. Clawson's (2009) *Level Three Leadership* contains an entire workbook section that is well worth implementing in that effort. Using the concept of gauges, it is also useful to leaders to utilize the concept of a dashboard for purposes of considering all seven dimensions collectively as well as focusing awareness on specifics.

Figure 2.6. Seventh Dimension Dashboard

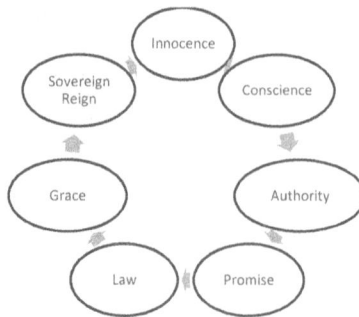

Source: Williams, 2016

By using a dashboard, *The Seventh Dimension of Leadership* can serve as a functional tool to measure various stages of growth in an executive coaching program. It makes tangible the otherwise abstract notion of innocence. Unlike the serpent's inquisition, the proper framing of questions and asking the right questions accommodates the presence of analytics in the administration of innocence. The advocacy for analytics accommodates two of the three key reasons for measuring presented by Hubbard (2014):

Figure 2.7. Reasons for Analytics

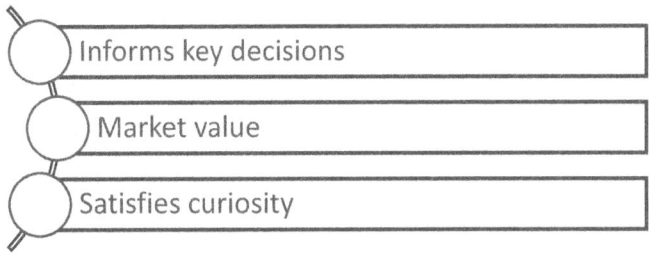

Informs key decisions

Market value

Satisfies curiosity

Source: Hubbard, 2014

While we could make a case for market value, it is the first and the third components of Hubbard's model that are best served by leaders who are willing to explore their relationship with innocence. Effective leaders are good stewards of their organizational resources; therefore, the usefulness of the dashboard and analytics allows for accountability to stakeholders and shareholders that exploring the seventh dimension of leadership is advantageous.

When we assess an administration that speaks to broken innocence, by default it includes the need to choose a model for change. Consider the following two sets of points that will become reference points for change. The first set of terms is:[xxxvi]:

Alpha change implies constant progress. It is sometimes associated with incremental change.

Beta change implies variable progress . . . The members change their vision of what should be and alter the course of the change effort itself.

Gamma change implies, besides beta change, a radical shift . . . It is sometimes called transformational change, a radical alteration from the status quo, a quantum leap or paradigm shift.

The second set of terms helpful to our exploration is[xxxvii]:

Figure 2.8. Terminology of Change

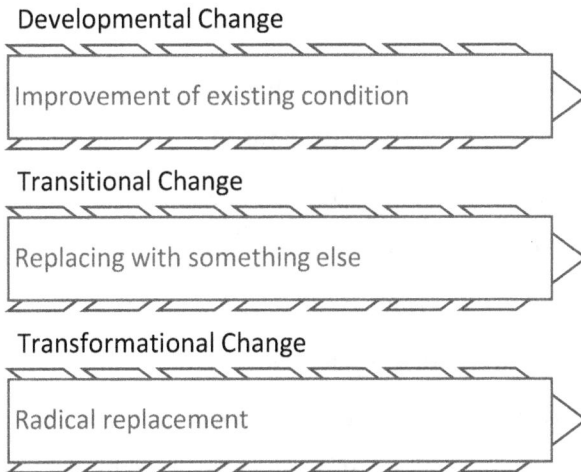

Developmental Change

> Improvement of existing condition

Transitional Change

> Replacing with something else

Transformational Change

> Radical replacement

Source: Rothwell, Stavros, & Sullivan, 2016

Those of us already in leadership must take on the burden of assisting those who have been violated in their innocence. Recovering workers who have had prior negative experiences is a viable mission in the 21st century world of work. Developing the field of talent management is a plus to the Human Resource Department. That may include retraining older HR personnel who have not yet shifted away from the "hire and fire" mentality of past years. As your company completes assessments with your leadership team, be sure to include the HR department. Remember that first impressions last forever, and your HR team is your organization's first impression for all employees.

Appreciate Inquiry (AI) is a viable model to use in the early stages of leadership development (and throughout our career). "Rather than focus on problems to be solved and gaps to be closed, they hypothesized that whatever you want more of already exists in an organization."[xxxviii] Having an unconditionally positive approach is the key to unlocking benefits to your group. Perspective is everything. Adam and Eve's departure from Eden can be viewed through the lens of displacement or through the lens of opportunity. AI utilizes a four-step filter:[xxxix]

Figure 2.9. Appreciate Inquiry Problem Solving

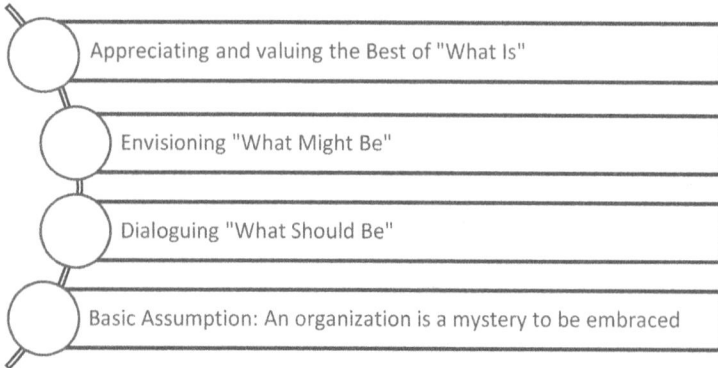

Appreciating and valuing the Best of "What Is"

Envisioning "What Might Be"

Dialoguing "What Should Be"

Basic Assumption: An organization is a mystery to be embraced

Source: Losey, Meisinger, & Ulrich, 2005

Appreciative Inquiry is a model that is perfectly compatible to the dispensation of innocence as its fundamental intent is to create destiny. Once destiny is unleashed, there is no turning back. Despite the multiple dispensations still waiting the Samaritan woman and you and I, once the cause is established, the end is secured. "Being confident of this very thing, that He who has begun a good work in you will complete it until the day of Jesus Christ." (Philippians 1:6). Let us continue our journey from innocence to sovereign reign.

Reading Between the Lines

One of the specific points for the breaking of my innocence took place in the 8th grade on a babysitting job when three of my classmates decided that they were going to "teach me how to be a girl." The sexual acts that resulted became my first significant secret of shame. One of my life principles is that I do not make excuses. I will offer an explanation, but I am not going to make excuses. When I was young, my lack of excuse-making meant that I was going to be out in the open and in your face. I strongly encourage reading Judith Viorst (1998) Necessary Losses as a tool for understanding the patterns of loss and healthy recovery. Several years ago, I had the opportunity to interact with the leader of the boys from the babysitting incident. It was with total peace that I walked up to him, shook his hand, and asked about his family. A few days later as I was driving to work, the Spirit of the Lord nudged me and said, "Don't act like you did something big because you forgave him." I immediately responded with, "What? Who me, Lord?" The next question from the Lord was, "Do I need to get out your list?" I am grateful for the abrupt slap that blocked self-righteousness from tainting the forgiveness.

The truth is that we have all offended someone in our lives (or more than one) when we had minimal means to fix what we did. In many cases, there is never the opportunity to apologize or offer any consolation for our actions. There are few of us that have not either had our innocence broken or been the person who broke the innocence of another person. Most likely, there is more than one incident in our lives, but the key to moving through dimensions is to identify moments or dynamics and recognize that we shifted from innocence to conscience. Effective leadership demands that we revisit our offenses and do all that is possible to make amends. For those who prefer, Steps 8-10 of any 12-step program address making amends and doing a personal inventory of wrongs we have committed. From the Qur'an, the concept of jihad is a struggle within that resolves the intentions of our lower self with the higher *purposes of spiritual destiny. Native Americans uphold the seven Grandfather Teachings which includes bravery. It is not only having a fearless heart but of doing what is right when the consequences might be unpleasant. Correcting the breaking of innocence is not simple or easy, but it is always worth the journey.*

Chapter 3

Second Dimension of Conscience

Please allow me to slow the pace just a bit. The United States is a strongly media-driven society that has contributed to a desensitization. Most of us can admit to eating supper in front of a television screen that is broadcasting injury and death. It is neither nauseating to us or even slows us down from the next bite or sip of our drink. We filter information in bursts of time. Not counting commercials, 30-minutes of news coverage includes death, war, weather, and sports. We barely flinch from hearing of a bombing in the Middle East to hearing that our favorite team lost their game the night before. Many read the scriptures with the same depersonalization to the events. For instance, the 28 words from 1 Kings 17:17 describe the death of a son. While I confess that I read rapidly, my timing for reading those 28 words was 3.78 seconds. Even if we triple that pace, it takes barely over 10 seconds of our life to read that the son was sick to the extent that the writer uses the Hebrew word *chazaq* which means hottest, hardening of the forehead or heart, severe – none of which is over in 10 seconds. It is an injustice to read those 28 words and has no sense of humanity about the son's suffering or the mother's grief.

Several years ago, I was praying about something. One night, I had a dream, and when I woke up, all I heard was the word *study*. I had the same dream the next night and the next. Each day, I had continued to pray about my situation. On the third night, I woke up and heard the word *study* again. Then I heard the Lord say, "Kathy, how do you like it when people put words in your mouth." Instantly, I said, "Oh, God, I hate it!" He said, "How do you think I feel?" What? What? Then I heard the Lord say, "Where did you hear the word study?" I said, "Lord, it is from 2 Timothy 2:15 that I should study to show myself approved." The Lord said, "Did I say study the Word, or did you just assume that I meant to study the Word because you read it in the Word?" "Lord, you have a point." The Lord said, "Study the dream. What were you doing in the dream? When you can answer that, you will have the answer to the prayer you have been praying." That same scripture tells us that the result of studying is that we would rightly divide the Word. One of the applications of the phrase *rightly divide* is a mining term which means to cut a new vein. We must consider the scripture with the intention of finding worth. We cannot mishandle the Word by merely skipping through its narration lightly as if it has no more impact than the evening news and a mix of sports, tragedy, and weather. The worth of knowing good and evil is the merit of conscience.

Here is a personal scenario that continues to build the case on not allowing our fast-paced world to cause us to miss the lessons of our experiences. My grandson Isaac died because he was born much too soon. He lived in the Neo-Natal Intensive Care Unit (ICU) of Riley Hospital in Indianapolis for 70 days. He lived in an incubator. He was born too soon to have a voice, so I never heard him cry. His entire hand could wrap around the tip of my little finger. On the day that he died, I held Isaac while the nurse periodically checked his heart rate to see how much closer he was to his final moment. From the time they removed Isaac from the equipment that sustained his tiny body to the moment the nurses took him from us, the clock had ticked for nearly 3,000 seconds. Every single one of those seconds held another level of letting go. Surely, we cannot so quickly move from innocence to conscience as if we had flipped the channels to avoid being bored by the commercials. Can you take a moment to reset the stage of the expulsion from Eden and put yourself in the script? Take time to write down answers to the following questions. What are the feelings? What are the fears? What is the plan? That quick scenario speaks volumes of where you are as a leader, particularly when faced with change or a crisis.

My Mom died of bone cancer at the end of 2015. For several months, her condition deteriorated in many ways. My Mom was my hero. She is the reason that I have a passion for reading and learning. What an amazing transformation to grow from the little girl who loved hearing her Mommy's voice with fingers pointing to the magical words on the pages to the moment that I became the voice of her books. One day while sitting with her, I asked, "Mom, would you like for me to read to you?" From her stack of books, I selected *Simple Abundance* (2005) by Sarah Ban Breathnach. In an entry titled "Fullness of Nothing," the author explains a concept from Japanese culture where negative space is not thought of as empty. ". . . empty spaces or the shroud of the unknown surrounding certain events is referred to in Japanese as *ma*, a word for which there is no English translation."[xl] The author's story is that she had cleared her living room mantle of familiar items. When her husband came home from work, he asked why the mantel was empty. She explained that it was not empty; it was merely full of nothing. We need to allow ourselves time between what was familiar and what will become the new positive space. In this case, negative does not mean undesirable. It merely means that we have made time to be full of nothing. As we move from one dispensation to the next and as our Samaritan woman moves from one relationship to the next, let us make time for being full of nothing. *By the way, when I finished reading, Mom said, "You read like you are on the stage!"*

Once Adam and Eve are removed from Eden, the first dispensation of innocence transitions to the dimension of conscience. They move from being the recipient of goodness to becoming the decision makers concerning good and evil. This dispensation (administration) concludes with the flood. The strength of conscience is having standards of right and wrong. The weakness of conscience is setting the standards by personal concepts. It is obvious that those of us who are living in the 21st century have distinct informational advantages over the biblical characters who lived the scenarios we use for introspection. ". . . conscience is an experience of a law not laid upon ourselves - a law written on the heart by God."[xli] The conscience is comprised of three zones:

Figure 3.0. Three Zones of Conscience

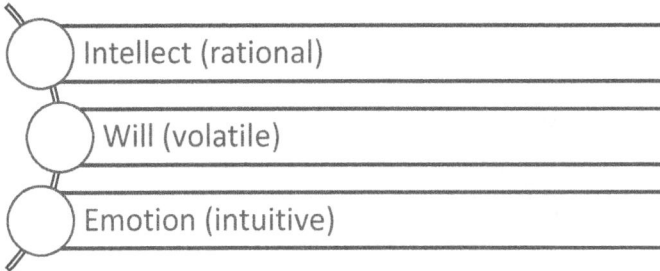

Intellect (rational)	
Will (volatile)	
Emotion (intuitive)	

Source: Hubbard, 2014

It is valuable to note that individuals might believe they are wrestling with the right or wrong of conscience when they are wrestling within the three zones of conscience. Example: The intellect may know the "right" of a decision while the will or emotion is still undecided. If we return to the woman at the well, in the dispensation of conscience, she is into her second marriage. What does the second husband represent, particularly in a leadership development analogy? In conversation with Jesus, his disciples asked why Moses had allowed remarriage? "He said to them, For your hardness of heart Moses allowed you to divorce your wives, but from the beginning, it was not so" (Matthew 19:8). The second husband represents social conscience altering spiritual conscience from what would have been a "no" to a "yes." If you are beyond your first marriage, please do not slam the book shut or toss it into the closest trash can. We are using this model to explore principles and not to judge. Remember that I am from the "power to the people" generation that burned bras in protest, smoked pot for creativity, and shacked up as proof that a piece of paper did not validate love.

When leaders assess conscience, it is both at a personal level and with a measure of their interactions with others. While scholars debate the exact number of years, we can safely pose that over 1,500 years took place between Adam's expulsion from Eden and the birth of Noah. Genesis 5:32 records that Noah was 500 years old when he became a father to his sons; therefore, we can conclude that the time between Eden and the Flood is approximately 2,000 years. Most of that time is within the dispensation of conscience. "The LORD saw that the wickedness of man was great in the earth and that every imagination of the thoughts of his heart was only evil continually" (Genesis 6:5). The word *heart* is interpreted as *conscience*. As our main character enters her second marriage, she is not grappling with only the consequences of choices. God has equipped her with a conscience. She did not just sit down and give up. She got up from a painful experience with a sense of what is right and wrong for her. We can imagine that as she has an opportunity for a second marriage, she enters the relationship with the sense that she will not repeat whatever resulted in the ending of a first marriage. The function of conscience is not intended for us to remain stuck in a could-have, should-have mode. Recognizing that conscience serves as an inner voice of reason gives way to welcoming Socrates' voice in our discussion.

Socratic questioning means that we add to ordinary questioning, "systematicity, depth, and a keen interest in assessing the truth or plausibility of things."[xlii] Leaders must develop the highest levels of thinking. An executive mode of thinking becomes an inner voice to, ". . . monitor, assess, and repair – in a more rational direction – our thinking, feelings, and action."[xliii] There are basic, universal standards to thinking and to think Socratically means that you understand how to assess questions that others are asking and to construct your own questions. It also means to evaluate domains of application. Does the question stir an answer that addresses one or more than one discipline or field of knowledge? Questions are an active part to Stephen Denning's (2007) three-step model for successful leadership communication:

Figure 3.1. Model for Leadership Communication

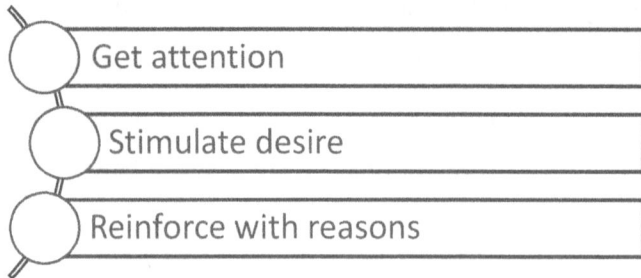

| Get attention |
| Stimulate desire |
| Reinforce with reasons |

Source: Denning, 2007

Decision making without process is stagnant and self-serving. It is a risky venture to depend solely on conscience for determining direction.

When we come to a place that correction of one season is determined by a personal definition of right and wrong, we expose ourselves to many complications. This book is not intended to become a Bible study. It is also not an advice column that supposes to fix or repair. I have long learned to tell people, "Some things cannot be fixed by one prayer or quoting a scripture or listening to a sermon." Most of us are like the lepers in the gospel that were "healed as they went" (Luke 17:14). Healing comes as we continue the journey. When we align our conscience to spiritual ideals and not our own standards, we have created a perfect setting for the birthing of ethics. Few of us get there easily or quickly. "We must be wary of substituting *eisegesis* (reading meaning *into* the Bible) for faithful *exegesis*."[xliv] We must also be cautious that we do not confuse conscience with innate socio-centric consciousness. "Innate sociocentrism says, 'It's true because we believe it' which worded another way, 'I assume that the dominant beliefs with the groups to which I belong are true even though I have never questioned the basis for these beliefs."[xlv] As moral beings, the compass of the conscience guides us to the paths that are acceptable to God and functional to us. Remember the many centuries that it took for humankind to arrive at a point that all God could conclude about them is that they did evil continually.

The Gap

We are not made aware of why the woman at the well is in her second marriage. Any number of scenarios are an option. It is not as important that we know the details of why she is in her second marriage so much as it is valuable to us to place ourselves in her story. Anytime there has been a first of something and then there is a second, there is a memory created. What we cannot afford to do is simply move on as if the first is no longer relevant. Ignoring is not a coping mechanism. "Avoiding a review of dynamics contributes to dysfunction. This applies no matter how or why the previous marriage relationship ended."[xlvi] There is a gap between what was and what is next. It is our processing in the gap that directs choice. When there is a loss, particularly when we were not in control of the variables, what happens in the gap? Do we pray? Do we drink? Do we seek counsel? Do we take more pills? Do we eat? How we comfort ourselves in the gap speaks volumes about our healthiness (or not) in a leadership role.

There is no perfection in leadership. It was never the goal, and it will never be the outcome. Adam and Eve made the decision to hide from God after their offense. Previously Adam took a walk with the Lord every evening. The day that he ate of the tree, he was a no-show for the evening stroll. Anything that disrupts an established relationship is problematic. Now, in the dispensation of conscience, the people are not only not hiding from God, but they have also made their wickedness a lifestyle with the belief that nothing can be done to them. We need only consider the 2008 fiasco of Wall Street to make the story current. Many executives thought themselves to be untouchable. That mindset did not begin in 2008 as that was merely the year that the ethical volcano exploded. The Sarbanes-Oxley Act of 2002 came because of the Enron scandal. "It has also prohibited practices that were previously regarded as retention strategies for key executives . . .."[xlvii] Conscience separates right from wrong based on present circumstance. Most likely, many contemporary names or those of recent generations quickly come to mind when we consider the corporate scandals within the past 10-20 years. Does your own name make the list? Your name might not have been media fodder, but how well are your standards aligning to accountability with a Higher Power? We are answerable for keeping a distinction between social conscience and spiritual conscience. Let us afford Adam and Eve some leeway for learning in the revised version of work they are operating in post-Eden.

> "If we were to contrast for a moment, however, the creation and eschatological visions of work in the Bible, we would say that in the creation accounts work is what human beings were fitted and commanded to do, whereas in the eschatological accounts it is what the Spirit inspires and gifts them to do . . .."[xlviii]

When we analyze and evaluate the concept of work and the roles of those within that notion, we must agree, "Work changes the world and imposes a new culture on what previously existed."[xlix] My youngest brother and his wife are both corporate executives. In a recent conversation, my brother and I were sharing about how the very circumstances that inspire us are sometimes those that exhaust us. He made a statement that captured my attention, "I didn't sign up for this, but I created this."

As leaders, we cannot afford to get so caught up in our own story that we use any circumstance to justify conditions and choices. We cannot and must not operate under the assumption that present efforts to not repeat past behavior or choices are the remedy that will move us successfully through the next dimension. In terms of actual second marriages, "It is, however, often based on the assumption that marital breakdown and divorce are the training grounds for a good subsequent marriage."[l] Restoration is a popular term in ministry, yet my advice to individuals is "If where you used to be was sufficient, you would not be where you are. Let's not make it a goal to become who you were." It is the inner soul of who we are that is the center of our self. When that becomes damaged or severely discouraged, the tendency is to lay aside the spiritual and search our natural environment for balance. Yet, the outcome of that strategy is a fragmented self. It is the healing of the soul that is our focus throughout the dimensions. "The soul is that entity within a person that integrates all of the components of a life into one's own, singular life."[li] In a counseling session with an individual who wanted to leave Christianity for another faith, the person finally said, "I might as well serve a fake god that I know cannot answer my prayers as to serve the real God who will not answer my prayers." What a powerful insight to discouragement! How many of us have been in that exact place where it seemed like the God who could answer our prayers simply does nothing?

Can you imagine approaching a colleague and asking for something only to hear them respond negatively? Sure, we can. All of us have been denied requests. Now, can you imagine trying to talk to someone who clearly hears us and responds with nothing at all? It doesn't take much to understand the hurt feelings that will result and eventually, aggravation and anger at feeling ignored. As a young believer, I used to say, "When I pray and don't hear God say anything, I am assuming He thinks my plan is all right." I am sure that I don't need to tell you how much trouble I caused myself with that thinking. Understanding the soul is not, by any means, a modern investigation. "Although soul was a cosmic principle for both Plato and Aristotle, their overwhelming concern was to understand the human soul. They knew all too well that things often go badly in human life, and they understood this to be, precisely, the result of a malfunction of the inner source of life."[lii]

Spirituality and the Conscience

We may propose that the conscience is contained within the soul as they have three compatible elements that make up their existence. Each is relative to the mind, the will, and the intellect. Why should modern leaders care about the soul? Workplace spirituality is rapidly coming to the forefront of essential considerations, including the Human Resource practice of talent management. Workplace spirituality can be defined as "... the recognition that employees have an inner life that nourishes and is nourished by meaningful work that takes place in the context of community."[liii] The days are gone where employees are satisfied making a living and going home with a paycheck. Today's workforce is seeking satisfaction, appreciation, and inclusion. Those characters cannot be found when people are left to individualized standards of conscience. "Conscience is not a principle or authority on its own but is assumed to act in a dynamic relation with the moral standards of society even when one is in good conscience dissenting from them."[liv] Conscience should serve as a gateway to self-reflection and self-awareness. Conscience becomes the voice of spirituality.

". . . workplace spirituality is defined as a framework of organizational values evidenced in the culture that promotes a process of finding meaning in the work process through relationships with oneself, others and the workplace community."[lv] The complexities of our modern workplace have caused employees to need decision-making skills that are not dependent on a hierarchical or authoritarian model of leadership. The multi-generational workforce has compelled leadership to reconsider how conscience is interpreted, and how that interpretation is applied to policies and procedures as well as influencing organizational culture.

Figure 3.2. Multigenerational U.S. Workforce

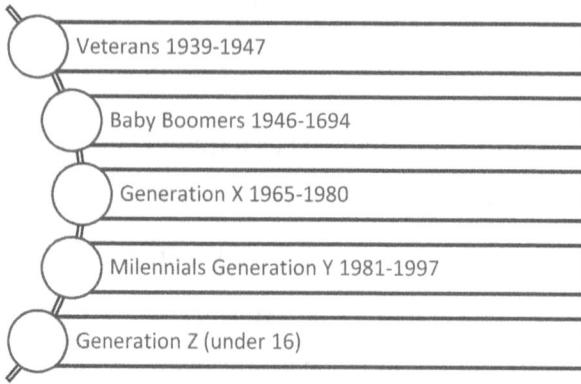

	Veterans 1939-1947
	Baby Boomers 1946-1694
	Generation X 1965-1980
	Milennials Generation Y 1981-1997
	Generation Z (under 16)

Source: Diversified Services, 2016

Different ages in the workplace are not what is new, although the presence of five generations in the American workforce is unique. "While the workforce has always been made up of multiple generations, the concept of shared values and workplace preferences as grouped by generation is a relatively new concept . . .."[lvi] A significant change in shared values is the job satisfaction motivators and the balance of work and personal life. Other major differences in the generations are the variation of leadership styles and the approach to conflict, innovation, and extrinsic versus intrinsic rewards. *Side note: My supervisor at the prison is younger than my youngest child; however, I can say that his age has never been a consideration for me. He is knowledgeable and deserves my respect and cooperation without consideration of age.* Moving through each dispensation and considering the life progression of the Samaritan woman, heartens gauging our own capacity for shifting and adjusting, not only for our own gratification but for shared values.

As we consider the woman at the well and her motives for entering a second marriage overlaid to the dispensation of conscience, we might conclude that she is aligning to the moral standards of society in her time. In weighing the pros and cons of conscience, contemporary leaders may find that they are aligning to expectations of society while internally dissenting from those same standards. We must exercise caution to not isolate conscience to the meaning typically determined by Western Christianity. "Certainly, there is no tidy definition, but it would be simplistic to reduce conscience wholly to personal integrity or cultural authenticity. Considering both Islam and the Christian West, it is arguable that conscience serves as a necessary foregrounding for engaging in the moral good in society by conviction rather than by coercion."[lvii] In Islam, the conscience is more in tune with internal legislative capacity than a person becoming their own moral counsel. Thus, both the woman at the well and modern leadership meet at the intersection of conscience for purposes of making right choices by having right intent.

Rather than wrapping conscience into a neat and tidy package of right and wrong, it exposes its owner to wrestling with a multiplicity of considerations. Do we operate out of individual conscience or collective conscience? Slave owners quoted scripture and felt that their conscience was clear. Abolitionists passionately opposed slavery based on conscience. Pro-choice advocates that a woman makes choices about her body based on her own conscience. Pro-life equally stands on conscience. The Vietnam War brought the phrase *conscientious objector* to the forefront. Egan (2010) offers some assistance in finding a balanced perception of conscience,

> "Conscience compels us to seek what is morally right so as to act morally and I in line with our deepest held beliefs. It is not simply a matter of taste. This is the act of informing our conscience: taking the time to find out what the moral issues are, what moral authorities [like the Church] teach on the matter. Then one is faced with the challenge of discerning the appropriate course of action."[lviii]

To apply conscience to contemporary leadership, particularly with current expectations of spirituality in the workplace, it is necessary that leaders are informed. Determining the appropriate course of action is met through knowledge and understanding of moral issues. Particularly in our global society with its cultural diversity and multi-generational workforce and stakeholders, this piece of the puzzle is essential. Otherwise, the simple right or wrong thinking of basic conscience has no lasting influence.

The dispensation of conscience began with an expulsion and ends with a devastating flood. The principle character known to most is Noah. There are several details to the flooding that are easily overlooked. For instance, most people believe that the animals boarded the ark in pairs. That is true, but not altogether true. Numerologists have much to say about the construction of the ark. There is an expression about "staying in your lane." Knowing that numerology is not my proficiency, it will take someone else's expertise to study that characteristic of the second dispensation. Genesis 6:19 and Genesis 7:9, 7:15 affirm that the animals boarded the ark in pairs, both male and female. The issue with conscience is that most decisions cannot be reduced to a mere "right" or "wrong." The black-and-white thinking of having only two options is not a viable personal or business approach to success. There must be an ambition to consider subsets of information. Genesis 7:2 details that of beasts that God has defined as clean, they are to come into the ark by sevens. Genesis 7:3 applies the same ratio to fowls. Noah's wife, his three sons, and the sons' wives joined Noah in the ark. Just like the woman at the well, the names of the women from the flood narrative are not given for the reader. We might interpret that as common to biblical culture, but that is too easy. Let's take the time to consider what else may be learned.

There are 187 women with names in the Bible, but there are hundreds who are not named. Many of those are known by their deeds while others are part of a collective assignment, e.g., genealogy. If we characterize Noah's wife, it is not a far stretch to imagine her as a strong woman, obviously dedicated to her husband and trusting that God did speak to him. Since she is not associated with the group that has grieved God, we presume that she is also living a righteous life which makes her a social anomaly among her peers. It is not easy to be different. Someone told me many years ago, "Before you start your professional career, be sure that you know what about you cannot be compromised." There must be a locus of control within each of us that is steady in a storm and persistent in turmoil. When everything around us is giving off glaring messages to go to the left or right, we should be dedicated to going the direction that is correct for our destiny. We find direction by alignment, not just to our own sense of right and wrong but to the internal mechanism set in divine relationship.

My knowledge is not nearly immense enough to delve into the scientific layers of creation. My supervisor and I had a conversation once where he expressed curiosity about the way that I think. He shared an observation that data supports many intelligent people do not believe in God but in scientific theories. Then he said, "You are an intelligent person, but it seems that the more you learn, the more it strengthens your faith." My response, "How smart am I really? I can't explain that wall (gesturing in his office)." To add to my list of "I don't know" I can include being baffled by a new moon and daylight savings time. According to Bill Nye the Science Guy, a compass works because the domains of magnetized iron lines up. Moving electrons within the earth's core cause the earth to become a giant magnet. "That magnetism is the same thing that makes compasses point north."[lix] Everything has a core or a center. Organizations and corporations have a vision statement. It is the fundamental reason for their existence. As leaders who are Christians, our core is the Creator God. It is His existence that centers us and gives purpose to all that we do.

Our conscience is not intended for us to make solo choices but serves as a compass that aligns us to the force we call God. Hence, our woman at the well receives an invitation to drink living water and to eliminate thirst. Jesus is extending an offer that she would align herself to a spiritual presence. The resulting order will heal the issues that have plagued her.

Jesus' interaction with the woman is an example of strategy as a learning process. He did not randomly choose the day, the time, or the setting. Nor was her witness to the men in the city unexpected. Perhaps, the whole scene at the well served as an intense training for the role she would play as a voice for the city. It contains all five of the elements proposed by The Center for Creative Leadership

Figure 3.3. Leadership Journey

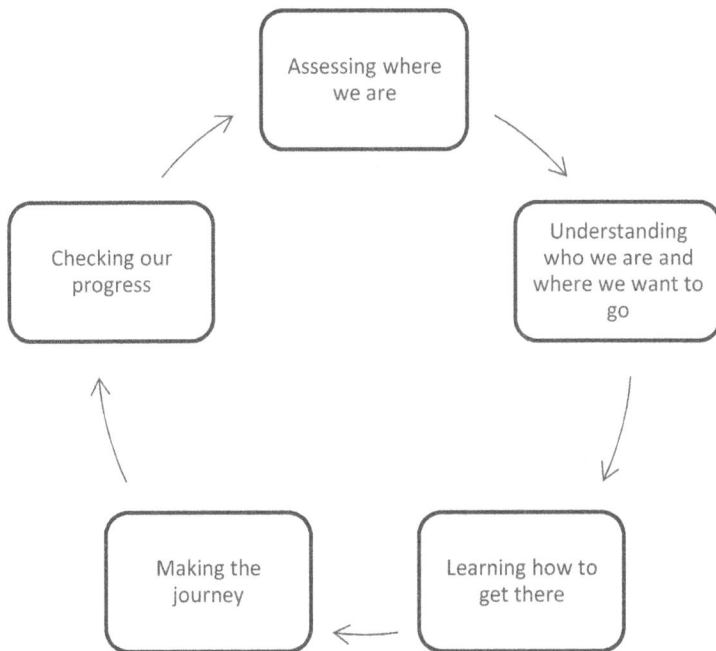

Source: Hughes, Colarelli, & Beatty, 2005

Remember that as we go through the dispensations, there may some that are more relevant to your personal journey than others. The various dispensations do not have to unfold in an exact order. It may be that only one will stand out to you and speak to your leadership progress. On the other hand, steps such as "assessing where we are" may not initially seem to include you until we dig further into the topic. Remember as well that the character of the woman at the well does not mean that this book is written specifying gender or marital status. Linear thinkers may not easily align with the concepts presented. "Linear thinking involves looking for (or assuming) cause-and-effect or sequential relationships between things . . .linear thinking cannot solve challenges in a nonlinear world."[lx] If you are a linear thinking, it sounds like the previous sentence merely dumped you on the side of the road. For the linear thinking readers, consider the difference between continuous change and disruptive change, implicit and explicit, and synthesis and analysis. It takes practice to incorporate other patterns of consideration. Remember that the objective is not to identify who is "right" and who is "wrong." This book is inclusive.

Application

Expanding on our use of a dashboard from the previous section on innocence, let us consider how to incorporate other tools for the administration of conscience. Dashboards are a way to analyze basic processes that collectively make something functional. Dashboards are also a visual tool for looking at associations between major variables. Conscience is a notion that is easily assumed to be present but is like the necessity of oil in a vehicle. With regular checkpoints, it is the substance that can result in a long life for a vehicle. With negligence, it quickly becomes the deterioration point causing irreversible damage. In a leadership coaching session, one of the activities relevant to the administration of conscience is the practice of centering. To the amateur eye, the physical size of a sumo wrestler seems to be his greatest asset; however, it is his ability to know his center of gravity and use that for inertia that is the strength of the art. Conscience is not always about overpowering reality with the black-and-white thinking of right and wrong but about knowing how to center.

One of the many tools available for leadership assessment is the Strategic Team Review and Action Tool (STRAT) offered by the Center for Creative Leadership. Using STRAT is intended as a mechanism for teams to consider how they process goals and objectives. One characteristic common between the woman at the well and the people of Noah's time is that neither seemed prepared with a strategy for the future. Their energy was expended toward the present. Our role as leaders who are Christians comes packaged with an anticipation for the future. Are we not waiting for the second coming of Christ? Luke 19 records a parable that Jesus told about a nobleman who went away but had the intentions of return. His instruction to his people was simple, "Occupy until I come" (Luke 19:13). His directive was that they should continue to do business until he came back. We are to operate in the instructions of that parable which give us the responsibility to make our world better until our King returns. Jesus also told a story about servants who were given talents by their master (Matthew 25:14-30). When the master returned, he was pleased with those who could return the original amount along with a Return on Investment (ROI). For the one who operated out of fear, the amount he originally had was taken from him, and to borrow from Donald Trump in *The Apprentice,* "You're fired." We are obligated to remain future oriented.

As we consider this topic, it is a reasonable point to suggest evaluating your organization's social media policies as well as technology policies. Most of us who have a Facebook page can attest that some of the content is outlandish. It is as if people have completely lost sight of the fact that they are exposing their words and pictures to the public. One of the aspects of working in a prison that I never lose sight of is, "There is nothing private in a prison." I work every day assuming that my emails are scrutinized, my phone calls are monitored, and my office is bugged by Internal Affairs. I assume with every conversation, that my words have the potential to be part of a grievance, if not a lawsuit. It might seem that such a mindset would feel oppressive, but quite the opposite. It has inspired me to refine my conversations and hold myself accountable to professional standards of communication. Particularly in light of the millennial generation's use of social media, executive teams are encouraged to revisit the "right" or "wrong" of public statements about the workplace. We need only consider Barack Obama's 2008 presidential campaign to grasp the potential of a social media platform. "In the years ahead, we may expect to learn more about how design features of particular social media (for example, Twitter's 140-character limit per message) encourage (or alternatively discourage) particular kinds of speech, and foster open and inclusive (or alternatively, closed and restrictive) discourse, among other concerns."[lxi] It may be in the near future, BRB, OMG, and IDK will be acceptable professional writing terms. Decision makers will also need to develop policy concerning "cloud" technology and outlining security expectations. The risks associated with hacking and violations of intellectual property add an extensive scope to conscience. All of this must be considered not just from a local company position but from a global perspective.

How do leaders deal with diversity and the varying definitions of right and wrong? A discussion that another chaplain and I have had many times over poses the difficult question of, "What do I do if my job requirements demand that I compromise my spiritual beliefs?" The simplest answer is to suggest a letter of resignation, but decision making is much more complex than that response. We cannot judge others if they are not operating in our brand of Christianity, particularly when we are discussing Westernization of Christianity. The concept of globalization is not meant to suggest a homogeneity. Particularly in this era of political correctness and the vulnerability to legal recourse, it seems that leaders must walk a fine line until they are on the verge of falling from something most of the time. Your primary allies in setting norms for your organization include your vision statement, the mission statement, and the code of conduct. Develop sessions of self-assessment for the leaders in your organization. You are a mentor to others as they explore the landscape of their thinking. "The endeavor is nothing short of evangelizing the mind. Accordingly, it requires surveying the intellectual territory and designing assignments appropriate to it."[lxii] Rather than examining the organization's vision statement, have your leadership team write a personal vision statement. "A person can have visions for different parts of his or her life, but a person's dominant vision can change or adjust other visions at any given time."[lxiii] Mission is the purpose that guides what we do each day. Sometimes we are so busy that we fail to recognize that our center has shifted and the clarity of what we view as right or wrong has shades of gray in it.

Reading Between the Lines

Conscience can be a thorny conversation. We like to think of it as our sense of right and wrong. It becomes a moral gyroscope, if you will, that will hopefully provide definition and balance. Any of us who have ever committed an infraction in life can tell you that the voice of conscience can be squelched. Repetition of a behavior seems to completely quiet the internal voice. Or does it? When I think back on the times that I made the choice to override that internal voice, I was always focused on the moment. I wanted what I wanted, and I wanted it right then. Perhaps conscience is not just about right or wrong but about sabotaging our readiness to move forward. We cash in the future for the present. As a young woman, I made terrible personal choices. It is only by the grace of God that I was never arrested. My Dad told me once, "If you decide to straighten your life up tomorrow, it will take you seven years to clean up the mess you have made."

My second son asked me once, "Mom, how is it that you were not racist? I know you grew up in racist times. Have you ever regretted having mixed kids?" I easily responded, "The thought of regretting you has never even formed in my mind." I followed with this, "That is not to say that I have no regrets. I was selfish and irresponsible and made choices with no regard as to their impact on others. That is what I regret, but I have never ever regretted my children." One of my brothers told me once that he believed God has given me the gift of people. My Mom told me, "You fascinate me, because you simply do not believe that you are better than anyone." My own failures keep a reality check on the faintest possibility of me ever thinking that I am better than anyone. Please know that I only tell the lighter stories that I believe people can handle.

For years, I did a lot of talking about what I was "going" to do. I was going to finish school. I was going to get a good job. I was going, going, going. Repeatedly I had to back pedal because my "going" never went anywhere. I remember one day telling myself, "Stop talking. Just shut up and do it." Living in the moment is a sure way to destroy your future. Without planning and strategy, there is no compass or map to get where you are going. Conscience is a tool for the future. Think bigger than using it to make a momentary choice. You can use a hammer to smash something, or you can use it to build something.

Chapter 4

Third Dimension of Authority

The dimension of authority is one of the more intriguing and complex matters. It began after the Flood and concluded at the Tower of Babel. The strength of authority is the assertion of control which implements order, direction, and purpose. The weakness of authority is the dormant compulsion toward rebellion and a false sense of control. This dispensation is also known as the dispensation of civil government. It becomes problematic within a few generations after the rescinding of the flood waters.

> "Failure to govern successfully appeared on the scene almost immediately, for Noah became drunk and incapable of ruling. Fellowship with man replaced fellowship with God."[lxiv]

Genesis 9:1 documents the instruction God gave to Noah and his sons to *be fruitful, multiply, and replenish the earth.* Genesis 9:7 offers more detail, "And you, be fruitful and multiply, bring forth abundantly on the earth and multiply in it." Genesis 10:32 confirms that initially, the command to populate the earth was met, "These are the families of the sons of Noah, according to their genealogies, in their nations; and from these the nations spread abroad on the earth after the flood." The pivot came when Genesis 11:2 establishes that in a migration, the people chose to settle in one location.

Let us make use of Genesis 11:2 as an analogy to a career path and the challenges of knowing when and how to transition versus the risk of staying in place. It is an unavoidable moment of decision in our modern workplace. "As research in neuroscience indicates, stress greatly reduces cognitive abilities. When our brain perceives unknown and potentially dangerous territories, it triggers instinctive protection mechanisms that greatly reduce our capacities to think and act rationally."[lxv] The assignment given to Noah and his sons included a decree that the animal world would live under the fear and dread of humanity. When we are not thinking rationally, we often reverse dynamics such that we become subject when we were intended to be in authority. Little wonder that the Apostle Paul encouraged the New Testament believer with, "For you did not receive the spirit of bondage again to fear, but you received the Spirit of adoption by whom we cry out, "Abba, Father" (Romans 8:15, NKJV). 2 Timothy 1:7 affirms, "For God has not given us a spirit of fear, but of power and of love and of a sound mind." While we can only surmise why the people halted their migration and chose to remain gathered in one place, we do know that the outcome of authority did not come to a positive conclusion for them.

Genesis 9:11 records a promise by God that He will never again destroy the earth by a flood. By the time we arrive at Genesis 11:1, the earth's population has become unified to the extent that the Bible records there was only one language. It is a curious factor in human nature that even in good times, we tend to be suspicious and prepare for our fears to actualize. Fear is mentioned in the scripture over 350 times. My list of fears includes snakes, mice, and anything else with a long tail. I heard someone suggest that most of us blame all snakes for what happened in Eden. Fear has a generalization energy to it that places all of one group or species in the same category. Traumatic life events tend to cause internal triggers that surface with the presence of like behaviors. The challenge is that similar behaviors do not always translate to similar motives or intent and can create further unnecessary trauma. Consider employees who have had negative interactions with a supervisor, and, in turn, trust no one in administration. Consider it on a national scale since 9/11 with assumptions that Middle Easterners are Muslims which generalizes to the accusation they are terrorists. Apparently, the fear that lurks behind unity is division as the people enacted a plan to outwit the potential for them to be scattered. It is fascinating that the entire narrative of Babel is contained in nine verses of scripture, yet volumes could be written about what might be learned from the scenario. The seriousness of their plan can be summarized by this, "By negating the value of the individual, the builders of the tower denied man's divine source and its attendant holiness. In so doing, they challenged God's authority as Creator."[lxvi] To deny the connection between God and humankind is to deny one's own nature. "One cannot deny the divine spirit in others without denying the divine spirit in all men."[lxvii]

Micromanagers (Control Freaks)

The first ambition of this writing is to serve as a guide to those in leadership to achieve a healthy balance for their own well-being. That agenda is no longer an elective for leaders to be effective for contemporary society, particularly bearing in mind diversity and the globalized economy. Without an inner balance, leaders become subject to fear in their decision making. Authority alone is insufficient, particularly to correct what conscience could not repair from broken innocence. Authority takes charge but as a solo entity, it lacks strategic wholeness. Because the initial effort to heal a breach of innocence by using conscience has become flawed, the people now decide to use authority or regulation to gather a sense of control. In its most extreme, leaders who prefer a mode of authority often have excessive issues with control. Put more simply, the question must be posed, "Are you a control freak?" To some extent, all of us struggle with this issue. In its extreme state, we can use our influence to convince entire groups to commit to building a tower to heaven. It is all right to admit that you have tendencies to micromanage (control freak), but it is not feasible to continue in that mode. The inability to let go becomes a cascading effect that permeates an organization.

"The final unintended consequence is that these senior leaders are the role models that others emulate. When control is tightly maintained at the top of the company, then leaders throughout the organization exhibit similar tendencies in their areas of focus."[lxviii] One of the negative outcomes of this mindset is the inadvertent, and perhaps unofficial, presence of a silo effect in your organization. Each department looks out for their best interest while slowly deteriorating the greater good for the organization. "The risk is, when we micromanage, when we don't allow for others to take the reins, we run the risk of stifling creativity, innovation and stamping out the independence and courage that allows a team (or teenager) to thrive."[lxix] Few of us have control issues exclusively at work. It typically translates to our personal life which becomes problematic in our wellness. Control expends energy that is ultimately exhausting to maintain.

> "While the degree may vary, most professionals are familiar with their inner control freak--that nagging feeling that if you want something done right, you have to do it yourself. It generally manifests as the micromanager, the overworked boss who has trouble delegating, the team member who takes over everything or the perfectionist worker who becomes trapped in the details."[lxx]

It becomes a state of hyper-vigilance with a root cause of feeling unsafe. We easily justify our control issues, because the same issues that becomes problematic is revered in our society, "Get control of it!" Being in control becomes an easy default mode, especially when surrounded by others who would rather not risk responsibility. If the "I'll just do it myself" mentality has become the standard, then you may want to consider this section a bit more closely. Here is a quick list of recommended strategies to counter a control mode:

Get over yourself. *Instead of finding all the reasons why you should micromanage, consider why you shouldn't.*

Let it go. *Start by looking at your to-do list to determine what low hanging fruit you can pass on to a team member.*

Give the "what" and not the "how." *When in doubt, share the "what" and ask (rather than tell) your team member about how they plan to get there.*

Expect to win (most of the time). *Be clear on what success looks like. Provide the resources, information, and support needed to meet those conditions.*[lxxi]

One of the inmates who worked as a clerk was a brilliant musician. He despaired of the gospel style of music or lively praise and worship. He and I had many conversations about why we were each drawn to a genre of Christian music. As we talked one day, he shared that in his childhood, his family was often homeless. He had slept in cars with his mom and brother. Alcoholism was a major problem in the family. There was always chaos. For him, the spontaneity of gospel music represented chaos. He had an intense fear of chaos. His love of traditional music and hymns was based in the orderliness and reliability that they represented. For me, the religion of my upbringing represented a stifling restrictive spiritual environment. I wanted the freedom of making choices and the liberty to explore life. Despite the rehearsal time that gospel music demands, there is always an element of spontaneity to its delivery. There are runs that take a one-syllable word and transforms it into six syllables and twelve notes (a bit of an exaggeration, but you get the point). For me, gospel music is like whitewater rafting. You get in the boat, but the river's energy directs the course. All our preferences have a root somewhere.

Learning to accept criticism is a skill. It reduces the need for being defensive or shifting into an authoritarian mode. For years when I would become frustrated, my retort was, "I'm not stupid." Finally, I had to not only examine that comment but recognize that me blurting out a defense about my learning ability was directly connected to a fear that I was stupid. I often advise people to spend a day listening to themselves. If need be, get a notebook and jot words and phrases down for later consideration. "The important thing with criticism, particularly with public attacks or even personal attacks, is to take a deep breath, listen to oneself, and listen to one's own reactions."[lxxii] Have an accountability partner – someone that you can ask, "Am I really like that?" We all need someone who will be nakedly honest and brutal if necessary, much more than we need someone who will try to ease our feelings. "Faithful are the wounds of a friend; profuse are the kisses of an enemy" (Proverbs 27:6).

Sometimes micromanaging is an unconscious defense mechanism. In the movie *Saving Mr. Banks* (2013), we hear the biographical story of Mary Poppins' author Pamela P.L. Travers. Her seemingly excessive control of Walt Disney's effort to make the movie *Mary Poppins* is rooted in her fear that her father will be considered a villainous and irresponsible man. "Only when he reaches into his own complicated childhood does Walt discover the truth about the ghosts that haunt Travers, and together, they set Mary Poppins free!"[lxxiii] Fear is a powerful mechanism and is often triggered by incidents that are beyond our reach to exchange but rarely do they exceed the grasp of repairing the outcome. We cannot trade our lives for anything other than our own, but we can expect that everything we experience has value to our forward journey.

Back to Babel

Let's look further at those who decided to build a tower that would reach the heavens. Do you recall that God had promised the people that there would never again be destruction by a flood? Yet, in the making of the tower, the construction consisted of slime as a waterproof material. We find the same material in Exodus 2:3 when Moses' mother put her son into the river as a plan to save his life. It is also the same material identified in Genesis 6:14 for the making of the ark. If the people trusted the word of God concerning floods, was there a need to waterproof the structure? Reconsider the statement from the section on micromanaging that the root cause of hypervigilance is a feeling of being unsafe. The people were doing well by going the direction God had set that they should populate the earth. Some event or conversation or other unknown specific variable triggered something such that the people stopped their movement and settled in Shinar. The one word that stands out in our observation is **settled**. Have you ever found yourself on a path, and then you settled? Hopefully, by the end of this book (or perhaps in the middle), you will be energized once again to blaze new trails.

The "they" of Genesis 11 is not given a specific identity, other than the previous references to the generations of Noah. We can reasonably assume that the "they" of Babel is comprised of Noah's descendants. Given the oral history tradition of ancient tribes, it is even more fascinating that the "they" of those who constructed the tower in Babel certainly were aware of God's promise and the history of mankind provoking God to a point of destruction. Perhaps our retrospective perception of their building effort is misunderstood. Perhaps the six words nestled amid verse four offers some clarity, ". . . let us make us a name . . .." The concept of having a *name* is equated to having glory, and God is unwavering on that point. He makes it clear that glory is reserved for Him and that mankind is incapable of being in the presence of His glory, much less to think themselves capable of being parallel to the glory. Oh, the mistakes we make when we strive to use authority as a tool for becoming like God. One missing leadership element from an administration of authority is counsel. "Authoritarianism operates on the assumption that an elite class of individuals has the right to exercise power and control over others by virtue of accumulated wealth, superior intelligence, or divine right."[lxxiv]

If we take a quick leap from ancient times to modern time, let us consider a fairly new model of leadership known as Wise Counsel Leadership. The four variables that influence the need for this model are information, competition, technology, and people. With the presence of the internet, employees no longer need to wait on administration to keep them informed. "Googling" can result in massive amounts of data at the fingertips of anyone with internet access. Global competition and the ease of access to e-commerce is part of the shift. Technology promotes a leveling of the playing field between executives and organizational members or stakeholders. People are far more equipped to make their own choices, rather than waiting on an instruction. How many television commercials empower patients to go to their physician and ask for specific medications rather than waiting on the doctor to make the decision? Spitzer (2008) suggests five necessary elements for a Wise Counsel Leadership structure:

Figure 4.0. Elements of Wise Counsel Leadership

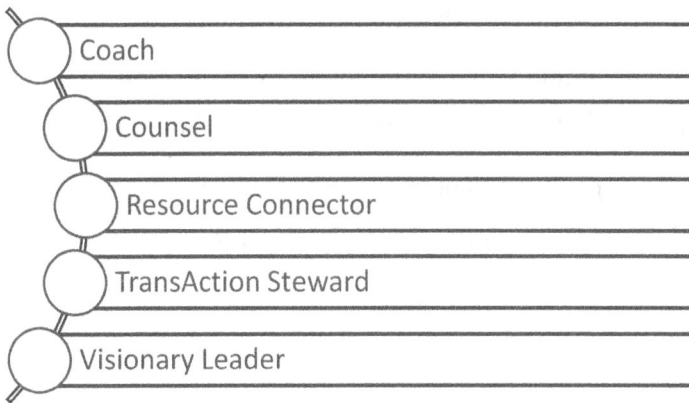

Coach

Counsel

Resource Connector

TransAction Steward

Visionary Leader

Source: Spitzer, 2008

A person who is operating in Wise Counsel Leadership does not attempt to impose solutions. Rather, they present opportunity for others to explore options and arrive at a decision. Visionary leaders are the ones who keep their eye on the horizon and encourage people to become self-directed. We should not feel threatened by someone's excellence. I often say, "Life is not a contest. If you are being the best you, and I am being the best me, then all is well."

As we consider the entire group of people that are engaged in the scheme to build the tower, we are given a setting to consider organizational dynamics. "Cultural values leave no fossils, making speculation unavoidable."[lxxv] Paleontologists would credit this generation of humankind with continuing to be in the rapid evolution phase; thereby making culture a valuable contributor to progression. "Scale increases opened possibilities for specialization."[lxxvi] For the group in the plain of Shinar, brick making is a specialty that will eventually become part of their captivity to the Egyptians. Geographically, Shinar is in ancient Babylonia, and its name means "two rivers." Water is essential to brickmaking to produce the mud as is the ability to grow straw to serve as the filler. Ancient brickmaking required kneading the mixture by walking on it for a period of four days in the initial phase and then re-kneading after the mixture has fermented. It was no small undertaking to consider producing enough brick to build a tower that would reach the heavens. When we consider the oral history tradition of ancient times, I cannot help but wonder if the enslaved Israel of Exodus 1:14 remembered the story of Babel as they were compelled to work with brick and mortar, ". . . and made their lives bitter with hard service."

Brief Interjection

Obviously working in a prison requires a certain level of authority. A tip I learned from another chaplain once is that if I am in a high-risk situation, my words need to be, "I am giving you a direct order to (fill in the blank). If the inmate does not comply, they are subject to a code of conduct report of defying a direct order. Only once in my years at the prison have I had to make a statement that strong and follow up with a radio call for assistance. An inmate had come into the chapel and, for the most part, was incoherent. He handed a piece of paper to me that had scriptures written on it about the end times. Suddenly, he started yelling at me to repent and told me I was going to hell and that my time was short. I stated, "Sir, I am giving you a direct order to stand still." He walked toward the door, and I called for assistance. Frankly, I was stunned at how quickly the emergency response team showed up in the Chapel, and, believe me, they secure the scene and then ask questions. There are situations where authority is the best avenue; however, it is typically situational versus an ongoing dynamic.

I have had many inmates look at me in amazement and say, "A female chaplain? I don't believe in women in ministry." My response is usually the same. "I understand that for many people, a woman in ministry is not what they are accustomed to from their denominational background. My belief is that when a woman is in authority over a man, she should do it with wisdom and not power." Please let me reiterate that authority is a complex topic as it is a positive dynamic in many settings, but can also complicate or halt progress when misapplied.

When my oldest son was a young adult, he still lived with me. At times, he and I had differences, and my response to him was typically, "Maybe it is time for you to have your own apartment. It is better that we are friends and you live down the street than for us to be enemies under the same roof." My logic seemed reasonable and considerate of my hope to have a good relationship with my son. One night in prayer, the Lord nudged *me, "I have an issue with you." The thought amazed me as I considered myself a decent person at that time in my life. When God finished talking to me, I was in a state of repentance. I am talking about the level of repentance where you lay on the floor in tears and ask only one question, "God, what do you want me to do?"*

The next day, I told my son, "I owe you an apology." I explained to him what God had let me see. As a mother, I was the first female relationship in my son's life. Our interactions built a foundation for how he would treat every girlfriend, and, eventually, his wife. When I made my comments about the option of him moving, what I was doing was instilling the message that when two people disagree, the man should leave. It did not matter that it was not my intention. The outcome outweighs intention. When we make mistakes as leaders (and oh yes, we will), we should own the accountability of it and apologize to those who were on the receiving end of our actions.

Cultural legitimation in ancient times was established by a direct relationship between the natural leader and the deity (or deities) of the people. In Genesis 1:26, man was created with two features assigned by God – image and likeness. To be made in His image is to have a resemblance and the likeness added similitude. In a later time, the prophet Isaiah hears God ask this question, ""To whom will you liken me and make me equal, and compare me, that we may be alike (Isaiah 46:5)? The people of Shinar might have benefited from hearing that question. The frailties of our bodies should be an easy discouragement to ever equating to God. The small shift from a normal temperature to a deadly fever or how rapidly we succumb to a lack of oxygen is a small example of our inadequacy to be equal to God. "Culture is a proximate mechanism of behavioral and symbolic selection at the group level."[lxxvii] Remember that the dispensation of authority came after the dimension of conscience; therefore, the culture collectively agreed that merely knowing right from wrong had proven to be deficient. They wanted what to go beyond the serpent's prompt in Eden of being *like* God (Genesis 3:5) and pursue equality with God.

It has been a longstanding habit of mine to read the Bible while asking this question, "What does this have to do with me?" That inquiry kept me grounded and made practical application of the Word a priority. *Practical* is likely the most accurate description of my ministry as it is important to have the listeners take something from the message that is useful to their daily lives.

If you have been in leadership for more than 24 hours (or less), it is likely that you have already discovered that authority alone is an insufficient exercise in directing others. As we overlay the woman at the well in her third marriage to the people planning a tower, we can identify points of intersection. They each have a history. Neither one has a history that is completely negative, yet each has taken steps to alleviate repeating undesirable outcomes. The woman and the people of Shinar have a rich spiritual heritage. Each is in an ironic circumstance, one at a personal level and the other at a societal level.

Figure 4.1. Comparison Graph

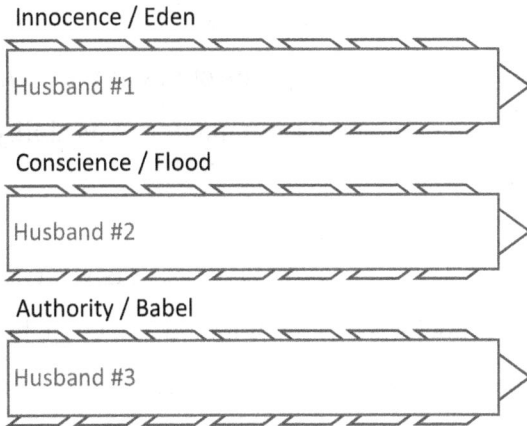

Innocence / Eden

Husband #1

Conscience / Flood

Husband #2

Authority / Babel

Husband #3

Source: Williams, 2016

One of the questions we need to ask is, "Would I have done it differently?" Perhaps in more detail, we might ask, "Could I have done it better?" In each case, we have the retroactive information available that empowers our response. Perhaps, then, the greater question is, "If someone else was me and had my history, would they make different decisions than I have made?" If we step outside of ourselves and pose third-party questions about our choices, would that be beneficial to effective decision making? The question is not farfetched at all but fits neatly into mental models of sense making. As a later study, it is worth investing in mapping the woman and the dispensations for the fit to sense making as, ". . . information does not exist externally as an object, but rather is being constructed by people . . . the study of information needs to be from the perspectives of the users themselves."[lxxviii] One aspect of sense making is its ability to deter the iatrogenic effect.

In layman's terms, the iatrogenic effect is what causes people to go to the doctor's office for a cold and come home with the flu. The same environment that facilitates healing often facilitates furthering the problem. "Iatrogenic . . . appear to be due to three sets of risk factors: (1) specific aspects of treatment . . ., (2) life context, and (3) personal factors . . .."[lxxix] As an isolated leadership framework, authority has all the risk factors that are suspect of causing the iatrogenic effect. An easy example is my work in the prison system. It is not uncommon to hear individuals profess that their incarceration, whether a county jail or a prison, has only sharpened their criminal skills. Tattoo artists are in high demand, and it is amazing what common items become tools of their trade. Inmates are not allowed to have click pens because the spring can be used as a needle. The motor in a computer that allows a CD/DVD drive to work also works as a motor for a tattooing gun. Unfortunately, we discovered that after an inmate(s) broke into the Chapel and took the motors from our computers. The people at Babel could have gathered their ideas to improve society or to infect one another with a mindset that proved to be their demise. More specifically, on the continuum that now includes innocence, conscience, and authority, the latter of the three in our setting at Babel proves insufficient to successfully alter the negative course that the people have taken. A plan to counter this outcome is found in the suggestion of identifying clusters of skills to identify competencies.[lxxx]

The dispensation of authority and the building of the tower is the perfect setting to consider innovation. Taking a counter view of the story gives way to suggesting that the people were simply innovative, and the tower was a means to have a higher order interaction with God. It might have been viewed as a creative prayer strategy. One flaw that may be considered in the approach taken is on innovative practices for prototyping. "The prototype becomes a medium for proving a point rather than a vehicle to evoke discussion."[lxxxi] If the people were truly striving to become closer to God, their approach was not one that opened a discussion. Schrege (2000) goes on to suggest that the longer the prototyping is under construction prior to meetings with senior management, the more likely it is ". . . that top management is being asked to approve – rather than participate in or react to. . .."[lxxxii] Something that Jews, Christians, and Muslims all have in common is the view of cosmology, ". . . there is one true and complete account of everything, namely what God knows."[lxxxiii] Accepting that God knows means that there is no way to devise a plan that excludes His presence.

Please pause for a commercial break. Kuhn (2012) states, "Textbooks thus begin by truncating the scientist's sense of his discipline's history and then proceed to supply a substitute for what they have eliminated."[lxxxiv] It borders on the "Who's on third base?" question of the 1930's comedy sketch by Bud Abbott and Lou Costello (easily "googled" if unfamiliar to you). This is a brief reminder that this book is not meant to be a brain teaser, a tongue twister, or a replacement for any other book on leadership. It is a voice at the discussion table. Its intention is not to offer solutions but to prompt dialogue. Back to our regularly scheduled programming.

If we consider the basic concept of *legitimate authority*, then it is apparent that both the woman and the people of Shinar are in that role. The function of authority implies the presence of compliance. There is an agreement between the one in authority and the one who is the recipient of the decisions of authority. Authority becomes the driver for social norms. We see that dynamic visible in the decision to build the tower, and in the decision to enter the third marriage. "Max Weber provides the seminal analysis of legitimacy as a descriptive concept, defining legitimacy as a belief in or orientation to the validity of a social order - one that involves the recognition that the rules governing behavior within that order are binding on its subjects."[lxxxv] One of the challenges of authority is that the holder of its power not translate authority to supremacy. The deficiency of authority that is initiated without the benefit of divine guidance is lacking. "Authority as grounded in reason has its rightful advocates. 'Truth' is here the watchword; truth is the ultimate authority. It requires no validation; its force is neither derived from nor enhanced by decrees of councils; it is not more true because found in the Scriptures, and its authentication does not depend on the fluctuating fervency of experience. It shines by its own clear light."[lxxxvi] The people of Shinar lacked truth, and Jesus' discussion with our woman at the well reveals the absence of truth in her experience.

One of the most fascinating insights about truth takes place at Jesus' trial when Pilate asks, "What is truth" (John 18:38)? Rather than waiting on a response, he turned to tell the Jews that he found no fault in Jesus. The scripture says that, "when he had said this" meaning that Pilate did not actually pose it is a question but more a statement. It reminds me of standing in the doorway of my children's bedroom, "Didn't I tell you to clean this room?" Obviously, I was not actually asking a question but making an observation based on a previous instruction to clean the room. The question more aptly could have been, "Why have you not cleaned this room?" In fact, Pilate's discourse with Jesus is based on a series of eleven questions.

Figure 4.2. Pilate's Questions

SCRIPTURE	QUESTION
John 18:29	"What accusation do you bring against this Man?"
John 18:33	"Are You the King of the Jews?"
John 18:35	Pilate answered, "Am I a Jew? Your own nation and the chief priests have delivered You to me. What have You done?"
John 18:37	Pilate therefore said to Him, "Are You a king then?"
John 18:38	Pilate said to Him, "What is truth?"
John 18:39	Do you therefore want me to release to you the King of the Jews?"
John 19:9	and said to Jesus, "Where are You from?
John 19:10	Then Pilate said to Him, "Are You not speaking to me? Do You not know that I have power to crucify You, and power to release You?"
John 19:15	"Shall I crucify your King?"

Source: Williams, 2016

The concept of questions from a paradigm of authority is vastly different than questions intending to spark dialogue. Recall any law enforcement television series, and, at some point, there is a scene in an interrogation room with a detective asking, "Where were you last night?" In that scenario, the detective has already determined the response he or she is expecting and any variation results in an intensified grilling. Responses other than the ones they want are rejected and replaced with deeper examination. "Jesus has positively asserted his identity, his purpose, and the nature of the community he offers. The audience awaits, but Pilate abruptly cuts off the dialogue with the question, "What is truth?" With this timeless question coupled with his immediate exit, Pilate refuses Jesus' offer by shutting himself off from its voice."[lxxxvii] Using the premise of questions that are not authentic maneuvers for exchange, we find a "what not to do" from the administration of authority. Few of us have not experienced a point (or more than one) in life where we asked a question without wanting a response or vice versa. Thankfully, the Samaritan woman embraces Jesus' insights about truth and its attachment to spirit and worship. At this point in her story, she is in relationship number three and has not yet arrived to the place where she could absorb his prompting. Life has demonstrated to me that deliverance or healing has a timing to it. Rushing that timing causes an immature experience that often must be repeated rather than allowing the lesson to take root. That is one of the reasons I tend to be extraordinarily patient with others. Paul's words to the Romans offer a balance of how we should consider others, "For by the grace given to me I bid every one among you not to think of himself more highly than he ought to think, but to think with sober judgment, each according to the measure of faith which God has assigned him" (Romans 12:3). Because we have had the opportunity to learn about a dimension of life does not mean we can measure everyone else by our progress. ""Blessed are the merciful, for they shall obtain mercy" (Matthew 5:7).

Application

As a leadership coach, the imperative is two-fold. The first piece is to engage leaders in a willingness to engage in transparency. What is it that the people of Shinar wanted to achieve? What did they feel was lacking that it seemed building a tower to heaven was their only option for achievement? When we consider a leader-follower relationship, we cannot view it through a one-way mirror. It must be a window where each party can see the other.

"Sawubona. It's an African Zulu greeting that means 'I see you.' It has a long oral history and it means more that our traditional 'hello.' It says, 'I see your personality. I see your humanity. I see your dignity and respect.' In the African village context, where everyone knows one another, it's an exceedingly powerful representation of understanding."[lxxxviii]

In the words of one of my mentors, "Sometimes the Lord is showing you what NOT to do." As we consider the third dimension of authority, some of the lessons to be learned are about what not to do. We must not use authority as blinders such that we do not see one another. Seeing others is a characteristic of psychological capital. When leaders empower their leader-follower relationship, it is inevitable that the outcome is positive reciprocity.

"Psychological empowerment consists of four dimensions as follows; (1) meaning, which define as congruence between the needs of one's work role and one's beliefs, values and behaviors; (2) competence, which refers to specific self-efficacy to one's work, or belief in one's capability to perform work activities; (3) self-determinant which define as a sense of choice in initiating and regulating one's action; and (3) impact which reflects the degree to which one's action can influence strategic, administrative, or operating outcomes at work."[lxxxix]

Transparency becomes a function of positive psychology which has two branches, positive organizational scholarship (POS) and positive organizational behavior (POB). "Positive psychology is a scientific study of the strengths and virtues that help individuals to realize their full potential and live a more prolific and meaningful life."[xc] Truth is a psychological construction as much as it is a set of factual interpretations. Modern leaders must not only know their own truth but have the capacity to aid others in having awareness of truth.

The second piece to be explored in coaching is problem solving. As we assess the challenges for the people of Shinar and the woman at the well, we can see that each of them became subject to a mindset. Leaders in the 21st century cannot afford to become embedded in a mindset. Problem solving must be a signature skill. "Signature skills may be acquired through schooling or experience, but they are the ones to which we bond our professional identity because we have *chosen* to do so."[xci] Problem solving falls under the umbrella of vision building. The formative life experiences of your leadership team must be included in exploring vision. Articulating vision becomes the guiding force for problem-solving strategy. A key to successful achieving vision and strategy is to identify partners and not participants which reverts to "I see you."

Retrospectively, we find value in the possibility that someone in Shinar should have asked the question, "Why are we doing this?" Questioning is the foundation of critical thinking skills. Bloom's Taxonomy is a worthwhile visualization to gauge the learning capacity of your organization, or, at least, your leadership team.

Figure 4.3. Bloom's Taxonomy of Learning

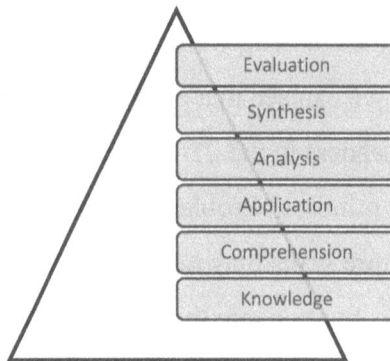

Evaluation
Synthesis
Analysis
Application
Comprehension
Knowledge

Source: Adams, 2015

As a leader, you are encouraged to use Bloom's model to accomplish two levels of achievement.

"First, use of the taxonomy encourages instructors to think of learning objectives in behavioral terms to consider what the learner can do as a result of the instruction. Second, considering learning goals in light of Bloom's taxonomy highlights the need for including learning objectives that require higher levels of cognitive skills that lead to deeper learning and transfer of knowledge and skills to a greater variety of tasks and contexts."[xcii]

If most your team is operating in the lower three levels of Bloom's, then it is worth considering whether you have an organizational culture of authority, or at least operate in an administration of authority. The question remains as to whether that is effectively taking your group where you are intended to go with the excellence that serves a 21st century vision.

Borrowing from *The Fifth Discipline Fieldbook* (1994), consider this set of questions toward creating a result and reflecting on vision:

- *I can't have what I want.*

- *I want what someone else wants.*
- *It doesn't matter what I want.*
- *I already know what I want.*
- *I am afraid of what I want.*
- *I don't know what I want.*
- *I know what I want, but I can't have it at work.*

Which of those questions frame your self-image as a leader? Operating merely in authority is a one-way venue, but honorable leadership requires a two-way street. Simple authority imposes itself on others, but expertise desires to share with interactions. Problem solving is a dynamic that must permeate all levels of stakeholders and organizational participants. "Less than 13 percent of American workers have ever received extensive training in how to do their work better."[xciii] Unfortunately, much of our workforce has been left to fend for themselves in the skills that improve performance. Problem solving has become an essential skill to our innovation-driven economy. Leaders must have vision and commitment to developing their workforce. "Personal mastery implies a willingness to invest in what is necessary to create an environment that helps employees become high-quality contributors."[xciv] The misinterpretation of authority places development in jeopardy. Once again, we embrace the value of learning what not to do. A glaring omission in the dispensation of authority is the absence of questions. Genesis 11:3 documents the decision to make bricks and Genesis 11:4 documents the decision to build the tower. Questions are not part of this dispensation which may be a valuable lesson for modern leadership. Let us not be guilty of enquiring, "What is truth" and simply moving on to the next task at hand.

Reading Between the Lines

One of the great challenges of living in authority is its propensity toward the need to be in charge. More than that, the need to be in charge is focused on not repeating the past rather than building relationships. When my oldest daughter was about 8-years old, she and I were walking to the laundry-mat. While I carried the basket of clothes, she carried a jug of detergent and a jug of bleach. As we walked, she swung her arms, and I repeatedly said, "Do not swing those jugs. If the cap comes off the bleach bottle, the bleach can hurt you. We kept walking, and she kept swinging her arms, when she suddenly asked me, "Mom, have you ever been embarrassed of having brown kids?" I pretended to be stunned and said, "Oh my goodness! I didn't even think about something until just now. I am white, and you are brown. I bet it is embarrassing at school to explain to your friends that I am your Mom. Is it embarrassing to have a white mom?" She said, "Oh no, I would never be embarrassed about you, Mom." My response was, "Besides, maybe I haven't always been a white woman." That caused her to completely stop on the sidewalk and say, "What? How can that happen?" I calmly continued, "Maybe I used to be a little Black girl, and my Mom told me to stop swinging the bleach bottle but I wouldn't listen." She poo-pooed me and said, "Oh that can't happen." (slight pause) "Can it?" Authority alone would have dismissed concern based on the leader's (or the Mom's) perception of its value. Strategic leadership provides a dependable relationship base that says, "I see you. I hear you. Your presence has worth." My daughter never had to wonder again if her mother was embarrassed at having brown children. The misuse of being in charge by authority would have provided an abrupt, "That is ridiculous" level of response that would deprive her of an interaction that gave closure to her uncertainty. Viable leadership willingly entertains questions and engages in dialogue.

Chapter 5

Fourth Dimension of Promise

The dimension of promise covers a period of approximately 470 years. In total, the dispensation of promise begins in Genesis 11:10 and concludes in Exodus 14, although some dispensationalists extend it to Exodus 19. In either case, the principal characters are contained within those passages. Within each dispensation, God assigns stewards of the administration. There are also specific responsibilities given to mankind in each of the dispensations. "The responsibility of the patriarchs was simply to believe and serve God, and God gave them every material and spiritual provision to encourage them to do this. The Promised Land was theirs, and blessing was theirs as long as they remained in the land."[xcv] Major characters during this dimension include Abraham, Isaac, Joseph, and Moses. The strength of promise is hope. The weakness of promise is vulnerability to violating commitment. While we can focus on how mistreated the Israelites were during their enslavement by Egypt, there is the unavoidable truth that they initiated the migration from their own land to Egypt. Integral leadership demands that we take responsibility for decisions that result in deeper turmoil. We will examine the details of this decision further into the chapter.

The woman at the well has developed an intriguing testimony by the time of her fourth husband. She has survived the breaking of innocence, the violation of conscience, and the disruption of authority. If nothing else, she is a role model of stamina and downright gutsiness. Like Israel entering Egypt, she is voluntarily entering this fourth relationship. For husband number four, she believes in the promise of anticipation. Have you ever met someone who seemed like their presence in your life was going to fix everything negative from your past? Have you been that person that felt that you had the capacity to bring healing to a series of offenses and harm? Perhaps you are in the role of the fourth husband where you had nothing to do with the issues of innocence, conscience, or authority for others, yet your presence is hinged to their past. If ever there was a time for a leader to pause and come to an understanding of their leadership style and capacity, this is the point! It is not enough for us, as leaders, to understand our style but to evaluate its relevancy. Is the approach we are taking meeting the needs of the objectives we have set?

Operating in promise is a sensitive area. In the hands of some, it becomes egotistical. The mention of ego is not an accusation toward someone as if they intentionally use promise for self-glorification. Few people approach leadership with intentionally devious motives. There are any number of dynamics that can draw a person astray. Here is a story about President Abraham Lincoln.

> "Abe Lincoln is supposed to have thrown a man out of his office after the man offered Abe a bribe. The bribe involved a substantial sum and Abe was really angry. His anger was directed at the man in question, but also at himself. He is reputed to have said, "Every man has his price and he was getting close to mine."[xcvi]

As leaders, we have a responsibility to recognize not only our shortcomings but when someone is getting close to our price.

An ongoing quandary for anyone in leadership is maintaining balance in relationships. A chaplain is often one of the few positive staff members that someone who is incarcerated has communication. We do not have to deal with the inmate's file or reentry program or conduct issues. We have the liberty of remaining optimistic. One of the young men who worked for us as a clerk told another staff member that everyone was rooting for him to be successful in his reentry. He made the mistake of telling the person, "Ms. Williams would let me live with her if she could." I fired him that same day. In that conversation, I told him, "If I did not have the respectable reputation that I do, I would already be sitting in Internal Affairs' office being grilled with questions about why you would say such a thing. Thankfully, my supervisor laughed when he heard what you said." It is a delicate balance to maintain professionalism when our character inadvertently becomes someone's point of promise. I am known for being pleasant and kind, but I am also known for following the rules. The chaplains have 15 inmate clerks. We interact with those men every single day for 8-hour shifts. It is a balance of remembering that even though we might talk about sports or other topics, they are incarcerated, and I am going to go home at the end of the day. I have a standard that I call being *personable* without being *personal*.

Brief Interjection

The reason I am so adamant about maintaining appropriate boundaries in the prison is not based on the notion of a prison but about the men who are striving for re-entry. Whether a man is incarcerated for drug dealing, robbery, larceny, or a sexual crime, they all have a common denominator – the lack of boundaries. In my time of working in a prison, I have known of several staff who were released due to either trafficking or personal relationship with an inmate. What message does that send? It tells men who are already struggling with boundary issues that healthy boundaries do not matter. The adverse message that embeds into an inmate is inexcusable from someone who was supposed to role model positive behaviors. We can lift that concept out of the prison setting and put it into any workplace setting. When people are trying to find hope in promise, leaders bear a weighty burden to maintain appropriate relationship.

That same message works both ways. When I worked in conflict resolution in the inner city, we dealt with a lot of young people who lived in horrendous situations. One young boy told us that he never sleeps in his bed. He sleeps on the floor in case bullets come through the windows. Staying low reduces the possibility of being struck by a stray bullet. A message that was consistently reinforced by the director of the center to staff was not to make excessive promises to the children. She would say, "One day, someone is going to offer you a better job with more pay, and you are going to take it. Be sure that when you leave, you have not become one more adult who has abandoned these kids."

The leader's role in a dispensation of promise is to develop *positive organizational scholarship* ". . . which concerns how organizations develop human strength, foster vitality, and resilience, and unlock potential."[xcvii] This dispensation, or administration, may be one of the most challenging. Remember that the people have been compelled to accept a worldview, unlike anything they have known. Whereas there were a common language and proximity, they are now scatted into diversity. If we consider modern theories, we can suggest that the scattering of the people was a positive response to their groupthink. Groupthink "occurs when group members become so enamored of seeking concurrence that the norm for consensus overrides the realistic appraisal of alternative courses of action . . .."[xcviii] One of the major weaknesses of groupthink is the rationalization to resist any assumptions that have been made. When the group decided to build a tower to heaven, there was nothing rational about that notion. Moses deals with groupthink several times during the Exodus. A leader who promoted *positive organizational scholarship* would have strategies to steer their energy to an attainable outcome.

A few years ago, a young inmate became ill which resulted in his death. My supervisor and I went to the housing unit to speak to the men who were clearly distraught over the loss of their friend. The men were so upset that I volunteered to arrange a special meeting in the Chapel that evening. When the men arrived, they were angry and grieving. Some of the comments made were about getting the administration to listen to them "no matter what it took" and going "old school" even if it meant taking hostages. Everything in me said it was a high risk to not call for security and release the meeting. I was mentally reviewing our training on hostage situations and planning my compliance with their requests. Instead, I continued listening and trusted that they needed to vent. One inmate Chapel clerk was in the meeting with me. After listening for a while, he calmly (and naively) said, "You know, if any of you are running a fever, you need to go to medical right away." The whole room froze. I wanted to put him in a choke hold and tape his mouth shut. What he said was needed, because the anger of the men about the other guy was not the core issue. The core issue is that nobody goes to prison expecting to die there. Their friend's death made them face the possibility that it could be them, and that was the most terrifying thought of all. When people are facing something that is new to them, fear is a common denominator. Have you developed the skills of identifying and addressing fear? It is an unavoidable leadership scenario and one that we must be prepared to meet.

Your capacity for managing distress, apprehension, and anxiety, is linked to your leadership style. This is not an optional discussion as recent data demonstrates that the U.S. economy absorbed $190 billion in healthcare costs due to workplace stress.[xcix] That is greater than the Gross Domestic Product (GDP) than most nations in the world. Depression is nearly 25 percent of the total in billions spent on healthcare.[c] Beginning with executive leadership and permeating throughout the organization, a communication campaign of both understanding and information will alleviate negative perceptions of depression. Understanding implications to the workplace and developing a response is vital.

"Unless organizational leaders clearly support efforts to protect and enhance workplace psychological health and safety (PH&S), there is little chance of making any lasting positive change. Leaders who understand the importance of PH&S will send a clear message regarding the urgency of these interventions, allocate sufficient resources to them, demonstrate the organization's commitment to change, and drive change when reluctance or resistance form barriers."[ci]

Thankfully, my workplace is not only sensitive to the issues in general, but my supervisor is also excellent about reminding the chaplains that we are caretakers; therefore, we need to take care of ourselves as well. In our monthly interdepartmental meetings, PH&S is a frequent topic of conversation. The executive team is particularly sensitive to holiday stress, seasonal depressive disorders, and the specificity of certain departments. For instance, we have a mental health area that houses over 100 men with serious mental illness. They live in individual cells and have heightened security measures for any sort of movement. Chaplains visit the area no less than once per week and walk through every one of the ranges of cells. Each time I leave the area, I whisper a prayer of gratitude, "Lord, thank you for allowing me to have a sound mind." My story could have switched with any of those men.

The first time I went into the Mental Health ranges, I was escorted by a custody officer who was a very large man. As we walked toward the cells, he said, "Chaplain, you are going to meet a guy that is going to tell you that you are an angel sent straight from heaven and that you are the most beautiful woman he has ever met in his life. Don't take it personally. He told me the same thing earlier this morning." One of the skills I developed from visiting those with serious mental illnesses is not to take it personally. Many of them do not remember what they said only minutes after they have said it. Then there are others, like one elderly inmate who asked me for a Bible. I declined his request as I had been warned ahead of time that the men in that area would ask for anything paper so that they could jam their toilet and flood their cell. When I told him that he could not have a Bible, he called me a b----- and started screaming for a Bible. I said, "Sir, there is nothing in my job description that says I have to be cursed, so our visit is over. I will see you next week." As I walked away, he was yelling, "Chaplain lady, I am sorry. Please come back." After speaking with every other man in that area, I went back and stood in front of his cell. "The very fact that you said that you are sorry says that you could have thought about what you said **before** you said it, so I will see you next week." The next week, I asked him up front, "Are you going to cuss at me this week?" He said that he would not and then proceeded to ask me for a Bible. Once I told him no, I quickly followed with a compliment, "You are doing well this week. I know you are angry with me, but so far you have not cussed. That is an improvement. How about if I stand here and read some scriptures to you? Then, I will take this Bible and give it to the officers to hold for you. We will put your name in it, and when you get your conduct levels raised, I promise that you can have it. Is that all right?" He was completely satisfied with our agreement.

Whether you started your career yesterday, have an interview scheduled tomorrow, or have been an executive for forty years, it is worth your time to consider leadership styles. While there are multiple leadership theories available for study, this writing will focus on the following:

Figure 5.0. Leadership Theories

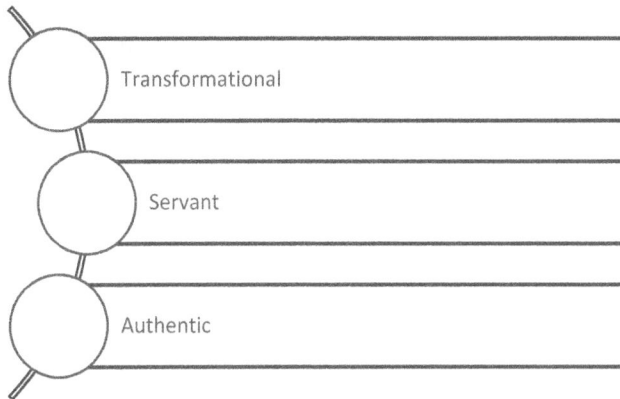

Transformational

Servant

Authentic

Source: Williams, 2016

Transformational leadership is a charismatic and visionary style. "It is concerned with emotions, values, ethics, standards, and long-term goals."[cii] Transformational leadership has proven to promote feedback from members of an organization or company. That level of exchange is critical to an administration of promise. "Transformational leaders respond to individual followers' needs by empowering them and by aligning the objectives and goals of the followers, the leader, the group, and the organization."[ciii] The benefit of that effort is the presence of emotional intelligence. Servant leaders consistently have a priority of considering the followers' best interests over their own. "Because servant leaders shift authority to those who are being led, they exercise less institutional power and control."[civ] One of the most striking statements that Robert Greenleaf (2008) makes about servant leadership is related to the prophetic. "The variable that marks some periods as barren and some as rich in prophetic vision is in the interest, the level of seeking, the responsiveness of the hearers."[cv] The tendency to highlight prophets in the scripture sometimes discounts the simplicity of Greenleaf's insight. Without reception by the hearers, the words of a prophet are meaningless. Servant leaders are cognizant of their hearers. Third on our list is authentic leadership with its intrapersonal perspective.

It is a recently developing theory and is a response to many of the economic and political catastrophes of recent years. It is a relationship style of leadership. Authenticity contains four distinct elements: awareness; unbiased processing; behavior; and relational orientation.

- *Awareness – relating to the self-knowledge of one's own emotions, cognitions, beliefs, and motives.*
- *Unbiased processing – meaning accuracy and objectivity with regards positive and negative self-relevant information.*
- *Behavior – based on the previous two and, therefore, genuinely self-congruent, and a*
- *Relational orientation – characterized by openness, honesty, and sincerity in one's relations with others. Within more traditional models, such as authoritarian and hierarchical modes of leadership, there is a theme of promise that can be woven universally through leadership.[cvi]*

Particularly when dealing with the sensitivity of promise, the leadership style is a relevant factor to consider. Of the three styles that have been highlighted, some of the descriptive terms include empowerment, alignment, hearing, and intrapersonal. All of us in leadership can benefit from periodically completing a fresh assessment. Recommendations include John Maxwell's Leadership Assessment, a Myers-Brigg Type Indicator (MBTI), a DISC profile and a relatively new test called Strength Finder. We need to not only know our style but the characteristics that make up the infrastructure of our style.

The expertise of Hackman and Johnson (2013) relate those as:

Figure 5.1. Leadership Characteristics

LEADERSHIP

How you work with others

Who you are

What you do

How you act

Source: Hackman & Johnson, 2013

A dispensation of promise is heavily dependent on communication. Quite interesting that the consequence of Babel is a scattering of people and a diversifying of language. As in previous dispensations, perspective becomes everything in either embracing opportunity that the change has presented or remaining stuck in what clearly has not worked to the group's benefit. The latter group, that we might label our curmudgeons, are ever present in any organization. Genesis 11:9 records that the Lord both confounded the language and scattered the people. The whole population had an immediate immersion program imposed on them. Anyone who has served as an expatriate for an organization surely is both empathetic and appreciative of their circumstance. Coupled closely with leadership style is organizational change facilitation. The ability to harness the energy of change is a high-level competency. Leadership style and change facilitation are the supportive forces to make promise actualize.

Promises have the capacity of setting goals and inspiring commitment. Googling the term *promise* delivered 439 million hits in .53 seconds. Shifting to Google images brought photos and clip art of the "pinkie promise." Merriam-Webster (online) says that promise means someone has given an assurance of something. For the first time in our dispensations, the word future is intertwined to the meaning of promise. In April 1945, President Harry Truman promised a national healthcare system. In 1964, President Lyndon Baines Johnson promised to eliminate poverty in the United States. In 1978, President Jimmy Carter promised to end the U.S. dependence on foreign oil. Did any of those presidents lie? No, the presence of the promise came bundled with a commitment of resources. Promise-making is a package deal. It comes with the responsibility of role modeling the character traits needed to achieve agreed-upon goals. In the prison, I supervise the Christian praise-and-worship ministry and often tell the men, "Many of the men in the congregation are making up their mind about what they think about God based on what they see in you." People make their choice about promise based on what they see in leadership.

A characteristic common to the Samaritan woman and Israel is their capacity to survive in difficulties. "But the more they afflicted them, the more they multiplied and grew" (Exodus 1:12). The administration of promise comes packaged with an examination of ethics and integrity. "Conventional wisdom has it that two of the most glaring examples of an academic oxymoron are the terms *business ethics* and *moral leadership.* Neither term carries credibility in popular culture . . . ."[cvii] We can assert that ethics was likely not a strong presence in the previous dispensation or the scenario at Babel would not have occurred. When we shift from an administration that lacks ethics to one that necessitates its presence, is the mission to create or rebuild? That is a question that modern leaders must ask as they seek to activate ethics into their leadership style and hopefully, into the organizational culture. The supportive dynamic for ethics is trust. Effectively engaging in promise is to put trust in a person's moral compass. "Trust is the framework within which emotions appear, their precondition, the structure of the world in which they operate."[cviii] Promise naturally triggers emotions, yet it is not to be confused with charisma. It is an expectation of improvement on prior circumstances and a commitment to a continuation of upgrading. "Putting ethics into practice requires not simply decision making, but accountable decision making."[cix]

As we consider the administration of promise, we can look at some critical decision-making points in the story. Once again, I must credit the Jewish group in the prison for opening my eyes to a fresh perspective of Joseph and his brothers. The men were in discussion about why there was such a lengthy period from the moment the brothers put Joseph into the pit until their reconciliation. Joseph was put into the pit in Genesis 37:20, and it is in Genesis 50:18 that they repented to Joseph. One of the men said, "God always gives us plenty of space to repent." Joseph's brothers had multiple opportunities that spanned many years to correct what they had done to Joseph, yet they chose to protect their dark secret. The dispensation of promise contains a space of time for the people to make right what they have done to violate innocence, conscience, and authority. By the way, Joseph's response to his brothers is one of the most powerful insights in the scripture. The Message Translation words his response, "[19] Joseph said to them, "Don't be afraid! I can't take God's place. [20] Even though you planned evil against me, God planned good to come out of it. This was to keep many people alive, as he is doing now." That is our ultimate hope in promise. Whatever others have done to us and whatever our own faults have become, what starts as evil can have a good ending if we recognize that God always had a plan. It is our responsibility to step into the plan and make sure that our growth becomes a benefit to others. Promise is by the nature of its definition an inclusive term.

Operating in promise develops humility. As a child, the library was my kingdom, and I was its queen. I often roamed its aisles simply staring at titles and making a connection to the treasures held within the covers. One of my favorite stories is

Homer's *Odyssey*. The cleverness of Odysseus to overthrow Penelope's suitors required him to be humble. By dressing as a beggar and allowing the people to make fun of him positioned him perfectly for the accomplishment thought possible only by Zeus. Odysseus did not identify himself by a medal or certification but by a scar. "As he spoke, he opened his rags to betray the great scar: and when the pair of them had studied it and knew it for sure, they wept . . .."[cx] Promise that lacks humility is problematic. Humility is, ". . . an interpersonal characteristic that emerges in social contexts and connotes (a) a willingness to view oneself accurately, (b) an appreciation of others' strengths and contributions, and (c) teachability."[cxi] The Apostle Paul understood, "For I say, through the grace given unto me, to every man that is among you, not to think *of himself* more highly than he ought to think; but to think soberly, according as God hath dealt to every man the measure of faith" (Romans 12:3). Humility becomes the balance of promise.

There is an undercurrent to the dispensation of promise that must be addressed. Recall that each dispensation (or administration) comes attached with specific stewards and unique responsibilities. In this dispensation, the primary responsibility was to remain in the Promised Land. A famine became the initial motivation for the Israelites to do business with Egypt. In the end, Jacob took not only his immediate household but all his family and descendants. According to Genesis 46:2-3, "And God spoke to Israel in visions of the night, and said, "Jacob, Jacob." And he said, "Here am I." Then he said, "I am God, the God of your father; do not be afraid to go down to Egypt; for I will there make of you a great nation." The last time we heard the promise of becoming a great nation is attached to Abraham. We also hear the promise of a great nation given to Ishmael in Genesis 17:20 and to Moses in Exodus 32:10. Duvall and Hays (2012) offer a list of fallacies that are common interpretive errors.

Figure 5.2. Word-Study Fallacies

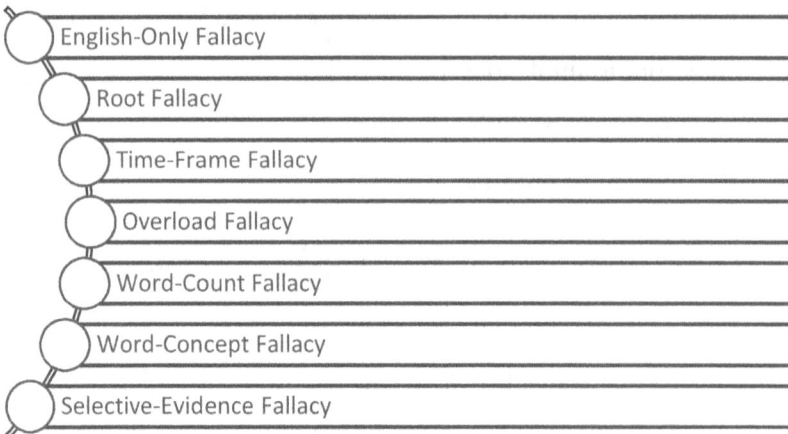

- English-Only Fallacy
- Root Fallacy
- Time-Frame Fallacy
- Overload Fallacy
- Word-Count Fallacy
- Word-Concept Fallacy
- Selective-Evidence Fallacy

Source: Duvall & Hays, 2012

As we consider the word *great*, we must not confuse it with our English notion of great as an intensifier of good or a pop culture perception such as the character Tony the Tiger in his description of Frosted Flakes breakfast cereal. The Hebrew *gadowl* includes large, distinguished, and older. When God warns to not be afraid, that is a road sign as to the situations ahead. God told Gideon to not be afraid (Judges 6:23), and Gideon faced an army with only 300 men. God told Daniel to not be afraid (Daniel 10:12), and Daniel faced a lion. He told Joseph not to be afraid (Matthew 1:20), and Joseph became the protector of Jesus and Mary. God did exactly as He promised as Israel became so large within Egypt that the ruling government feared them. That became the premise for enslaving Israel. They clearly were distinguished as their accomplishments in slavery are among the Wonders of the World to this day. There is no question that they became older, including a span of over 400 years before they transitioned to liberation. The relevance of this to modern leadership is that we must be aware that our ambitions and destiny do not often come into existence by our playbook. As a young adult, I had more than one mature believer speak these words into my life, "God is going to use you to do great things." If you knew my whole story, I assure you that it would be a challenge to connect the word *great* to my development. I dare not boast of being distinguished, but God has enlarged my territory, and clearly, I am older.

Application

Rather than a coaching session or a consultant's report, this section might call for a white paper. I asked my brother once, "As an executive, what is the difference between a consultant's report and a white paper for you?" He told me that a consultant's report offers suggestions to him, but a white paper sets policies. One of my professors expanded on that idea and stated that a white paper should be applicable in an industry and not simply a specific company. As a leader, the responsibility of decision-making stops at your desk. Assessments are essential to measuring the potential of your team. It is a multi-billion-dollar business to provide training for leaders. "Despite the huge investment by organizations, an increasing number of studies have been showing that leaders have not been performing well in their leadership capacities. The role of IQ has been questioned and the demand for answers has led to the proliferation of studies on emotional intelligence (EI)."[cxii] Experts have taken the study of EI into the field of neurobiology with evidence that emotions are directly involved in complex decision making. For purposes of this conversation, EI is summarized to be the awareness of one's own emotions and of those around us.

The expectation of assessments should be framed as complimentary and not a tool for criticizing. Scheduling assessment for your leadership team is a statement of investing in their value and one of transparency for the organization. The outcome is relative to executive coaching for those with lower EI or utilizing those with high EI in mentoring others. It sets a standard in your organization as to what the expectation is of EI levels for those in your organization at various levels of management or leadership. It is to be taken seriously as experts now gauge EI as a valued indicator of leadership performance above expertise, knowledge, or competence. "Emotional intelligence encompasses abilities such as being able to motivate one's self and persist in the face of frustrations; to control impulse and delay gratification; to regulate one's moods and keep distress from swamping the ability to think; to empathize and to hope."[cxiii] Promoting practices of EI reduces your organization's stress-related healthcare expenses, retraining leaders who are faltering in this area, and the overall well-being of your organizational culture.

Sidebar: Levels of Bondage

Before we go into the fifth dimension of law, allow me to interject a supportive exploration concerning bondage. Let us consider three levels of bondage: (1) captivity, (2) imprisonment, and (3) slavery.

Figure 5.3. Three Levels of Bondage

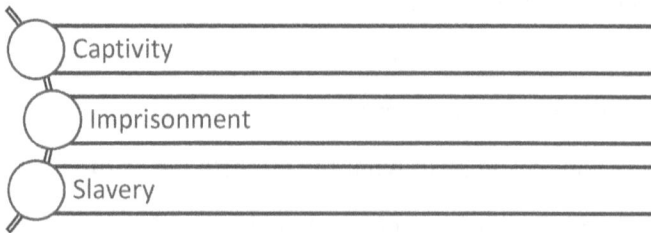

| Captivity |
| Imprisonment |
| Slavery |

Source: Williams, 2016

There are three variables present in captivity:

1. *There is a shift in your ruling government.*
2. *The new government becomes your permission.*
3. *It is possible to still have social mobility and even prosperity but it is completely dependent on one of two factors – either your cooperation with the new system or favor.*

Daniel represents captivity. But Daniel resolved not to defile himself . . ." (Daniel 1:8). Daniel did not become a consumer of the systems. The word defile is ga'al which means impure or contamination or desecrate. We often hear the term "consecrate" in the church world but to desecrate means to reverse your positioning by participating in the unclean. To be taken captive in the scripture means to be lead away or to be removed from what is familiar and relocated in a territory that is governed by opposing forces. Captivity can take place in your mind. It does not necessarily mean a physical location. A person can be captive in their body, soul, or spirit. Paul's instruction in Ephesians 6:10-18 offers a dual offensive-defensive strategy concerning spiritual captivity.

For our contemporary world, we look further into the concept of captivity. "But I see another law in my members, warring against the law of my mind, and bringing me into captivity to the law of sin which is in my members" (Romans 7:23). The Greek word captivity speaks to capturing the mind or domination by charm or traits with irresistible appeal. In other words, the captor seems to speak our language. What brought captivity? The shifting of a lifestyle. Mesmerize the mind and all else will follow.

There are two variables present with imprisonment:

1. *There is a sentence by the ruling government*
2. *The ruling government becomes your supply and your economy*

The Hebrew word for prison speaks to your household, dwelling, descendants, and household affairs. Breaking imprisonment is to break its clutches on your descendants and your household affairs. The root of the Hebrew speaks of building and establishing. A person drawn into imprisonment will have a much more difficult time being free. The United States fits this profile in regard to issues such as addictions (both prescription and illegal drugs). Imprisonment declares the foundation has been redefined. Aspects of life that would have been your responsibility for decision making are now dictated by those who are in ruling position. In the narrative of Joseph (Book of Genesis), he never lost faith in his dreams. Perhaps that is the hope that our woman at the well has for her life. Perhaps that is what kept her trying again and again in relationships despite all socio-cultural standards that said she should just give up. "When the son of man comes, will he find faith in the earth" (Luke 18:8)? Jesus greatest rebuke to his followers was "O ye of little faith."

Faith breaks the imprisonment of sickness, poverty, and death. Faith breaks the imprisonment of being ruled by law over spirit and of being ruled by religion and tradition over the Word. Jesus told people that their faith saved them, made them whole, and restored life to death. His prayer for his followers was that their faith would not fail. Back to our Ephesians prayer, Paul instructions, "above all take the shield of faith." Faith is a conviction of truth about our relationship to God. When we believe, all things are possible.

There are two primary variables present with slavery:

1. *The ruling government dictates your lifestyle and your portion*
2. *Any profitable venture coming from you benefits only the ruling government*

Slaves in the scripture refer to a united society and that can cast a shadow. The biblical narrative includes nations selling themselves into slavery when their ability for provision became so desperate that they could no longer see a way to wait on God. The Revelation reference to slaves is an after-effect of the crushing of Babylon (Revelation 18). The very name Babylon speaks to confusion. Those that seem to speak well have agendas of evil. Those that speak progress are agents of corruption. We see that right now in our political, educational, judicial, economical, and social systems. The progression shows that captivity takes individuals while imprisonment includes households and descendants until slavery overrules society. What breaks slavery? Prophecy. Every time that Israel was shifted from slavery to freedom, there was a prophet who led the cause. Little wonder then that the enemy would desire to break hope in the prophetic. It is the key to escaping slavery.

Reading Between the Lines

The fourth dimension is a challenge to consider at a personal level. One of my observations about life is that, "There is a fine line between faith and fantasy." Promise could easily fall in that sentence. Promise revives hope that something good is on its way. As Sam Cooke said, "It's been a long time coming, but a change is gonna come." My fourth relationship was not with a man, but with another woman. In fact, relationships four and five were same-sex relationships. Just like our woman in Samaria, the season of promise came because of violated innocence, disrupted conscience, and scattered authority. I have a humorous diagnosis that I call PTCD – Post Traumatic Church Disorder. My addictive personality had placed 150 percent of my energy into being a good person through the church, but God wanted me to learn to be a good person through Him. "I can do all things THROUGH Christ which strengthens me" (Philippians 4:13). Jesus said that He had to go THROUGH Samaria. Promise is something that we are supposed to go through but not confuse it with covenant relationship. Promise has purpose but not permanency.

*As a chaplain, most people do not cuss around me, or they hold their language when I show up. One evening as I was walking toward someone's office, I heard what my mother would have called "cussing a blue streak." I knew the staff would be embarrassed if I walked in, so I used my humor and hollered, "Hold the f-bombs! Chaplain approaching!" One day, one of the staff members told me that I should get on her motorcycle with her. I told her that was never going to happen because I was afraid of motorcycles. She told me how much fun she and her husband had on their rides, and she **promised** me that she would be safe with me. I still hesitated, and she blurted out, "Come on! You can get on behind me and be my b-----." I paused and said, "I have* *discovered that the world is a better place if I remain single." I still think that is one of the funniest episodes from working at the prison.*

Chapter 6

Fifth Dimension of Law

The dimension of law began with Israel's bondage in Egypt and ends at Calvary with the death of Jesus Christ. The strength of law is its firmness and uncompromising definition. Law brings order, but it can be misused for control. The law is not to be confused with boundaries. The first mention of law in the scripture is Genesis 47:6 when Joseph made it a law that one-fifth of all that Israelites' crops would go to Pharaoh. The law, as a prescriptive model, was intended to show appreciation for the gift of seed and as a proactive measure against future famine. Once the law becomes reactive, it takes on a contradictory nature to its original intent. In the dispensation of innocence, it seems that natural law was an implicit arrangement between God and man. It is only after mankind has stumbled in conscience, authority, and promise that the necessity of written law sets a new precedent. We may also suggest that law, known as the Ten Commandments, are present as a counter measure to the aftermath of Israel's captivity. It appears that law is a mechanism that God implements to undergird liberation. Let us take a brief detour into the journey from slavery to the point of law in Israel's history.

In the movie, *Uncommon Valor* (1983), Gene Hackman's character (Col. Rhodes) leads a group of Vietnam Veterans into North Vietnam on a mission to find POW's, including Rhodes' son. In a memorable scene where the American POW's are in an underground cage, one of the veterans extends his hand and tells the Americans that they are going home. With a confused look, the colonel's son speaks in Vietnamese and draws away from his rescuers. The power of that moment speaks to how comprehensively assimilated we can become to captivity of any kind. 2 Corinthians 10:4 reminds us that the weapons of our warfare are not carnal. We are not in an earthly battle; therefore, we cannot have earthly weapons. The weapons we do have can pull down strongholds. It has been my observation that something that qualifies as a stronghold is like a scene in *Uncommon Valor*. The sentence has been commuted. The rescue is at hand. The prison doors are open, but the person inside cowers and continues to speak the language of captivity rather than to walk out to freedom.

Brief Interjection

When I was a kid, my brothers and I played with magnets. One of the games was with the magnet and paper clips. We carefully lowered the magnet to see how close the magnet could get before the paper clips started jumping and attaching to it. We tried to make the paper clips spin and swirl on the table, or we put the magnet under the surface and watched the magnets move under the control of the unseen force. Have you ever sincerely loved God and still struggled with your carnal nature? Have you ever been faithful to everything you know to do and still find yourself swerving to the left or the right or wondering why certain people or activities seem to leap up and attach to you?

The reason that a magnet works is because the electrons have been lined up with a density at the atomic level that is called a line of force.[cxiv] Do you know that when you make certain choices again and again, that those choices begin to line up in your soul and develop a drawing power? Some choices have such a strong compulsion, that it does not take repeated interaction with it to establish that line of force. Even one connection can cause the attachment, e.g. pornography, addictions.

To demagnetize can happen in a few different ways. One is to heat the magnet which disrupts that line of force. No wonder that the scripture says to count it all joy when trials come (James 1:2) because it is our struggles that draws the characteristics of God and disrupts the negative lines of force. The prophet Malachi tells us, "But who may abide the day of his coming? and who shall stand when he appears? for he **is** *like a refiner's fire, and like fullers' soap" (Malachi 3:2). Think of the Bible stories where great transformation happened in a person after an exposure to a situation involving fire, including Abraham, Moses, and Daniel. Some of us have come to appreciate the fires of life that broke our attraction to various attachments.*

Understanding the intention of the law is key to activation of law. "The language of biblical law reflects the cognitive structures of its oral origins: it is to be read narratively rather than semantically, in terms of the typical images it evokes and tacit social evaluations (including values) with which those images are (culturally, socially) associated."[cxv] The Book of Leviticus not only gives standards for the people to follow but the definition for the regulations. For instance, with the dietary law, they were given specifics of the forbidden species such as chewing the cud or cloven hoof. The law is not intended to be merely a universal set of do not's but to provide definition. The unspoken partner to law is justice which God entrusts to humanity. Once again, an expert discussion of ancient law far exceeds either the intentions or the abilities of this writer. It is not helpful for the writing to take a sharp turn into a scholarly debate such the outcome is no more than an elaborate book report. The usefulness of law as a dispensation is a sequential step in the journey to sovereign reign. The issue is not always law but the application. Is it useful as a social philosophy, a literary concept, or legal theory? Do we have to consider an either-or approach or is there a collaboration possible?

The woman at the well speaks to Jesus through the lens of social norms, but is that law? Orthodox Jews of the time accepted that the Samaritans were considered "less than" Jewish because of their racial mixing. Sometimes we take social context and incorporate it into our spiritual framework until it seems that it is both law and is understood by all parties. I have heard many seasoned Christians use the quote "the eyes are the window of the soul" as if it is biblical. That expression is, in fact, attributed to Leonardo da Vinci as well as Shakespeare and others, but it is not in the Bible. "Money is the root of all evil" is another distortion of scriptural accuracy. Ultimately, the law should serve to move us toward definition and boundaries. Can you imagine the need for definition in the life of our Samaritan woman? While second, and even third, marriages have become common in Western society, the fifth marriage will typically raise eyebrows even for liberals. How does one arrive at a fifth marriage without internalizing the question, "What's wrong with me?" To some degree, law takes the burden of decision-making away from us as our primary role becomes compliance. Law becomes a distant but realistic enforcer. For example, I have no idea who authored the legislation concerning stop signs nor do I even know why the stop sign has the shape that it does. I only glance at it and know that compliance is my responsibility. One of the risks of an administration by law is a separation between the legislators (leaders) and citizens (members of an organization).

In Judaism, there is no separation of moral law and cultic law. "Holiness is enacted through the avoidance of defiling foods (Leviticus 11), but also through the pursuit of fairness, honesty, and justice in all dealings with other people (Leviticus 19)."[cxvi] The intention of law was not for paranoia but for awareness. The principles of honor and shame are woven throughout a culture of law. A dynamic of broken law is conflict – both internal and external. There is a difference between what the law says and what the law-breaker intends. Whenever I teach conflict, I like to use M&M's candy. As a little trivia, did you know that M&M's is war candy? The candy carries the initials of Forest Mars and

Bruce Murrie. The patent for the candy was awarded in 1941 and was initially given to troops in World War II. After the war, returning soldiers wanted more, so the candy was marketed to the public.[cxvii] The reason that I use the candy is to illustrate three levels of conflict – material, mental, moral. The first level of conflict is based simply on not having enough of something, e.g. time, money, or some other resource. The second level is based on psychological needs of acceptance, love, inclusion, and so on. The third level of conflict is a violation of what we consider right or wrong, good or bad. If two (or more) parties are in conflict, the resolution will only come if they are addressing the same level(s) of conflict. For instance, when one gang member shoots another, it may strictly be a material issue (turf, drugs) while society views it at a moral level.

As a chaplain in a prison, it has long been a curiosity of mine as to why the men choose various religious groups. "What gives a man peace (or a hiding place) through different faith practices?" It is particularly curious to me how men who are incarcerated for violating the law find spiritual peace by adhering to spiritual practices that are grounded in law. That curiosity is compounded when incarceration is the result of a sexual crime. I took the time to analyze each of our religious groups to see if there is a common theme of the crimes for those groups. The conclusion was an astounding "yes" for the pattern. The reason for not pursuing that project is out of concern that it would be used to be prejudicial against certain faith groups. But let us return to our woman at the well as we are deep into our dispensations. There are times that the interpretation and application of law places a focus on secondary rather than primary factors. It is the lens we choose that speaks most clearly to us and not necessarily the other party. "John tells us the time of day to explain why Jesus would be hot and tired, not to comment on when virtuous women drew water."[cxviii] Jesus' ministry is based on meeting the needs of the people who crossed paths with Him. He raised the dead. He healed the sick. In the case of this woman, He engaged in a conversation about worship. We have no other clues about her interest in worship, other than Jesus' divine nature connecting to her internal character.

The fifth dispensation (administration) of law is not rooted in enforcement but definition. When expectations come short over and over, we become muddled in our identity. The presence of law is an equalizer. In theory, it places everyone on the same terms. Because we have the benefit of retrospect, we know that this dispensation was no more the solution to the woman's issues than the first dispensation. We do not grow from profiling others. We grow from profiling ourselves. How would you fit into this dimension of leadership? A painfully obvious yet distasteful conversation that we need to have is to address the truth that most of us (all of us?) are control freaks at heart. Swift and decisive decision making is an admirable quality, but what if it is a need for control? Can we have an effective means if there is a defective intention? Control freaks always have a reason for not delegating. There is always justification for getting others to comply with their terms. ""It is the psychology of our ancestors, our parents, and grandparents, of our teachers and leaders, of almost all the people we know or know about. Coercion, to try and get our way, has been with us so long that it is considered common sense...we neither care where it came from nor question its validity."[cxix] The implementation of law and the application of law can be easily misunderstood. We need to look no further than considering the rules of our homes during childhood. We did not know (or appreciate) why our parents determined that there should be a set bedtime or demands of brushing our teeth and so on. We just knew that the application of rules inconvenienced our preference to do what we want.

It is a worthwhile detour in our journey to consider the notion of external control. Surely, our main character is experiencing the pressure of others believing they know what is best for her, particularly in a fifth marriage. Even if all four previous husbands died, it begins to raise questions about anyone having enough courage to enter a marriage with her. ". . . visible, short-term gains of External Control Psychology (ECP) are always easier to identify than the long-term losses."[cxx] Gaining another husband may have resolved the present concerns of being a single woman, but did it heal the underlying issues? As leaders, it is imperative that we are willing to search our motives and ask the hard questions. What is your next step if the answer is difficult? Options are considered in the "Application" section of this chapter. One of the inconveniences of the dispensation (administration) of law is its tendency to highlight enforcement. Consequently, it seems that its purpose is an immediate and present influence. Law, like the policies and procedures of an organization, can seem to exclusively serve as a control mechanism.

During the dispensation of law, our major characters are the people of Israel during and after their enslavement by Egypt. The people have assimilated to the culture of captivity that they are uncertain and resistant to Moses' presence as a liberator. The major obstacle in the exodus journey is the people's grumbling about the responsibilities of freedom. Their first recourse was to demand a return to captivity which had become their normalcy. There are always those who qualify as curmudgeons in every organized group. Those are the individuals who seem to disagree as a hobby. As a manager for public housing, one of my sections of apartments housed mostly elderly residents. One lady was known for arguing with just about everything and everyone. I dreaded to hear that she was in the office. She could have made curmudgeons qualify as their own species. One day, this person was griping about the children who played on the playground that was in the center of her block. I offered to relocate her to another area of the complex. Her answer completely changed my perception of her. She said, "No! I don't want to move! Having these arguments keeps me alive! I love it when the kids come." After that, I looked forward to our encounters as bantering was her personal exercise regime. There is a fascinating statement made by the Israelites in Exodus 14:12, "Is not this what we said to you in Egypt, 'Let us alone and let us serve the Egyptians' (RSV)? Is it that the Israelites did not want their liberation, or is it the case that the curmudgeons simply have the boldest (and the loudest) voice in the crowd?

It can be a challenge to remember that the resistant people in your organization are typically not the majority. In the world of marketing, we would find those individuals in the latter part of the adaptation bell curve. Borrowing some numbers from technology adaptors, we find the following graph to be the typical rate of saturation:

Figure 6.0. Market Adaptation Scale

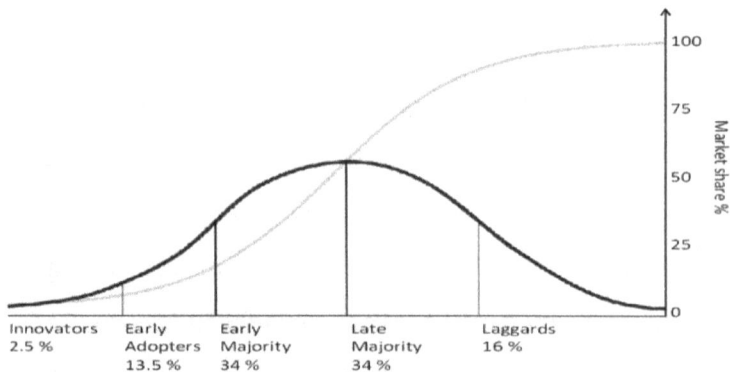

Source: Digital Marketing Website, 2016

It is the responsibility of an effective leader to close the gap between these mindsets. Particularly when significant change is on the horizon, the leader as change agent must have a strategy that will acknowledge the difference in acceptance while simultaneously resolving those same differences. The primary tools available to a leader are engagement and communication.

Perhaps there was a bit of curmudgeon that had developed in our woman at the well. Remember that all Jesus said was, "Give me a drink." Instead of a *yes* or *no* response, she retorted with ""How is it that you, a Jew, ask a drink of me, a woman of Samaria?" For Jews have no dealings with Samaritans" (John 4:9, RSV). When Jesus attempted to pull her back into the conversation about water, she made a practical observation ""Sir, you have nothing to draw with, and the well is deep; where do you get that living water" (John 4:11) followed by a historical stance, "Are you greater than our father Jacob, who gave us the well, and drank from it himself, and his sons, and his cattle" (John 4:12)? Her conversation with Jesus broke every social norm, yet it established a new norm. It provided an option that law does not possess – Spirit. When the woman left Jesus, she makes an intriguing statement to others, ""Come, see a man who told me all that I ever did . . ." (John 4:29). It is in this statement that we hear her take responsibility for the marriage choices which she connects to every other choice she has made. While law provided an avenue for the relationships in her life, she expresses a void that has now been filled by the inclusion of Spirit. Spirit makes sense of what the law can only regulate.

While the dispensations are also considered administrations of time, they can also be viewed through the lens of culture. The world at the time of the woman at the well as well as Moses leading the people was based on a culture of law. "Culture is an abstraction, yet the forces that are created in social and organizational situations deriving from culture are powerful. If we don't understand the operation of these forces, we become victim to them."[cxxi] Drawing from the lessons of this dispensation and translating them to modern leadership requires the successful construction of culture. Like law, culture can become so deeply embedded in a group that it is most noticeable when it is violated. The woman's first response to Jesus about the inappropriateness of their conversation was based in culture, yet it had become such a strong presence that it was an unspoken rule (law).

When a staff member in a prison wants to speak to an inmate, the staff member writes a pass for the person. The pass is delivered to the inmate's location, and the officer in charge of that area releases the inmate per the date and time noted on the pass. Although the passes were secured in my office, writing the pass was a task that I frequently delegated to a clerk. The clerks are inmates who have secured a job in our department. Our facility hired a new chaplain who came to us from another prison. He noted my habit of having a clerk write out the pass (still needing my signature to be authentic) and reported me to our supervisor. When we had a face-to-face conversation about the incident, his position was entirely based from a security perspective while mine was based from a clerical perspective. For me, the writing of passes was simply a clerical task. For him, it was an opportunity for a clerk to misuse a pass and cause a security issue. Who was right? Who was wrong? Neither of us. We simply had two different perspectives of a task. Another factor is that he had experience in a maximum-security facility while my experience was based on a medium-security facility. The environment of enforcement was different. Each of our experience levels was valid.

It is worthwhile to note that when we are speaking of law, the difference in experience and environment will influence how an individual prioritizes its enforcement. The order of events for most organizations is a vision, mission, and strategy. A strategy of law is a guarantee to complicating fulfilling a vision or mission. The law does not reward. After driving for nearly 50 years, I have yet to receive any certificates from the State of Indiana for not shooting anyone or burglarizing a business. Systems of law lack reward mechanisms, or does it? If we consider both extrinsic and intrinsic rewards, my lack of receiving a certificate is resolved by my gratification of being a good citizen. More than any other time in history, the issue of extrinsic and intrinsic reward systems is on the table for most, if not all, organizations.

Policies and procedures are nested within strategy to ensure consistency. Strategy is the driver and not the passenger of policies and procedures. Strategy is also a learning process; therefore, it must by dynamic and fluid. Law is a static definition, albeit it can be modified via a legislative process. Utilizing the expertise of The Center for Creative Leadership, we can visualize strategy as a learning process with this graphic.

Figure 6.1. Strategy as a Learning Process

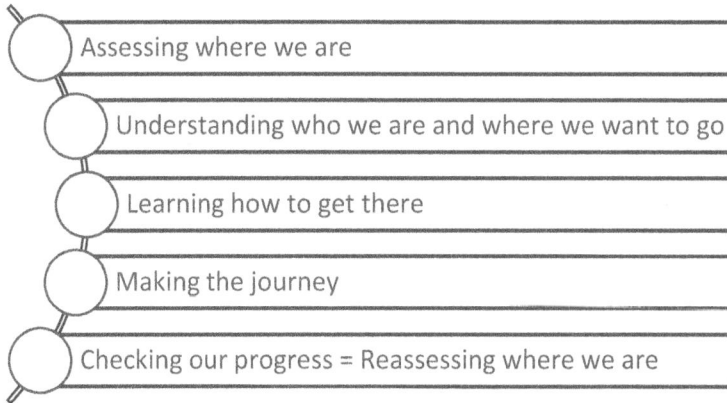

Assessing where we are
Understanding who we are and where we want to go
Learning how to get there
Making the journey
Checking our progress = Reassessing where we are

Source: Van Velsor, McCauley, & Ruderman, 2010

Reassessing where we are in our discussion of dispensations is the point that transitions from law to grace. There is a point where it must be validated that where we have been will not suffice to continue the journey. Remember that law is a stabilizer. For the Israelites, they needed the structure and security that law provided. They were liberated from captivity, so they needed a definition to their current conditions. It is reasonable to suggest that our woman at the well also needed some stability as her world had shifted from innocence to conscience to authority to promise, all concluding with devastation to her sense of normalcy. The fifth husband representing law gave her space to find refuge. Effective strategy understands how to make policies and procedures compatible with the current vision. "As such, developing vision, strategy, and policies in support of sustainability is a key element of success."[cxxii] Remember that Moses was the original visionary and the recipient of law, but it was his successor Joshua who moved the people from the wandering to the promise of occupation. There must be a point of application to prove the effectiveness (or lack thereof) of law as an administration.

It is not the diminishing of law that brought grace. Jesus alleviated the fears of the religious community. The Message reads, "Don't suppose for a minute that I have come to demolish the Scriptures—either God's Law or the Prophets. I'm not here to demolish but to complete. I am going to put it all together, pull it all together in a vast panorama" (Matthew 5:17, MSG). The Complete Jewish Bible reads, ""Don't think that I have come to abolish the *Torah* or the Prophets. I have come not to abolish but to complete" (Matthew 5:17). Footnotes to the 1599 Geneva Bible read, "Christ came not to bring any new way of righteousness and salvation into the world, but to fulfill that in deed which was shadowed by the figures of the Law, by delivering men through grace from the curse of the Law: and moreover, to teach the true use of obedience which the Law appointed, and to engrave in our hearts the force of obedience."[cxxiii] The law provides the brush strokes to paint the canvas of grace. It is the technique that the artist uses that brings to life the panorama Jesus describes in Matthew 5:17.

The question persists, "What am I gaining from reading this book that provides fresh insight?" A consultant with over 40 years' experience told me, "It is your job as a consultant to make the client think about things differently."

As you consider your role in developing and implementing policies and procedures, recognize that you are writing a fluid document. Beyond its fluidity, let your framing documents serve a prophetic role in your organization. That does not necessarily equate to a spiritual role but a role of insight with a continual vein of futuristic planning. It can be summarized as being mindful. Mindfulness is a ". . . preoccupation with updating."[cxxiv] You are not just a leader; you are an organizational development practitioner. As I considered the topic for my master's thesis, I settled on the following, *Rethinking the Indiana Sex Offender Registry Relative to Parole Stipulations and the Indiana Department of Corrections.* In a visit to the prison's Assistant Superintendent, I said, "I don't know what I was thinking to take on this project. I am just a chaplain." She immediately corrected me and stated, "You are not JUST a chaplain. You are a corrections' professional." Adding those two words to my vocabulary transformed my self-view. It is your mindfulness that becomes the guiding light for your organization. "When we are mindful, we implicitly or explicitly:

1. View a situation from several perspectives,
2. See information presented in the situation as novel,
3. Attend to the context in which we are perceiving the information, and eventually
4. Create new categories through which this information may be understood."[cxxv]

You are the one choosing the filter or special effects on the lens through which those around you will look.

How do we balance the collective and individual nature or what we do? In the prison where I serve, the majority are serving sentences for felony sexual crimes. Let me ask a simple question, "When you hear the term *sex offender*, what comes to mind?" The key that I have found is this, "Let every man be his own story." It is not possible to gather those with such crimes under one umbrella concept. When the population began to transition to sex offenders, one man asked me, "Did you have any reservation about working with sex offenders?" I said, "Not at all" but then I had to admit, "Wait, yes, I did have a reservation. I asked God if I had something to give." As a leader in an organization, let every person be their own story. The path to achieving that mindset is through mindfulness of your own story. Remember that an administration of law is an administration of definition. How do you measure in self-awareness when it comes to sense-making and meaning?

Figure 6.2. Sense-Making and Meaning

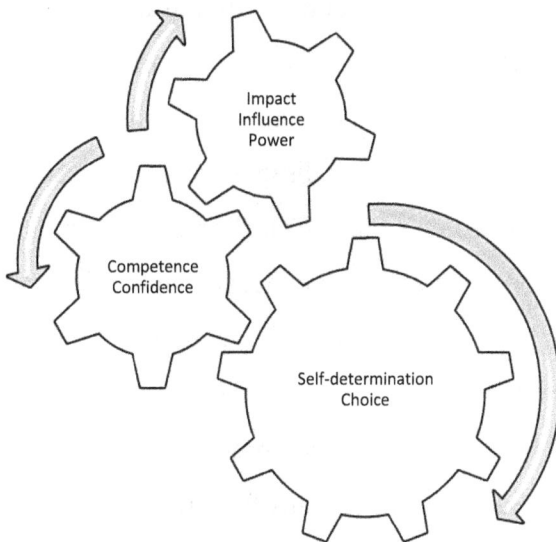

Source: Van Velsor, McCauley, & Ruderman, 2010

It is only when we practice mindfulness for self that we can take initiatives that develop self-awareness in others. The dispensation of law as an administration is an opportunity for self-awareness. Do I steal? Do I commit adultery? Do I covet what belongs to others? If I put those questions into the workplace, there is an easy transition. Do I comply with policies and procedures? Do I operate in ethics and integrity? Do I align with the company code of conduct? Do I take ink pens home? Am I using my work email for personal business? Am I part of the negative gossip about colleagues? Another aspect of law is the decision between condemnation or conviction. Condemnation is an externally-applied sense of wrong, while conviction is an internally-driven sense of wrong. For many years, I had only condemnation concerning abortion. The church disapproved, so I disapproved. My position was based on someone else's stance, more specifically someone in authority. When my youngest daughter became a teenager, I bought a book for her about Christian character and adolescence. In that book was a chapter on abortion with vivid explanations of how various abortion procedures took place. I was horrified at the idea of sucking a fetus from the womb and tearing it into pieces (one of several techniques). From that day forward, I had a conviction about abortion.

I ask every person I see at work, "How are you today?" One day, one of my coworkers said, "Not so good today, Chap." I asked what was wrong and should have taken a clue from her response that, "A man that has been like a father-in-law to me just died." I asked if she why she was at work, and she responded that she was okay. Seeing her the next day, I said, "My goodness, what are you doing here?" She told me it was complicated. At first, I thought her emotional coping mechanism was like a baseball player that gets hit with a line drive and puts up their hand to let others know to just leave them alone while they shake it off. The next time I saw the young lady, I said, "I owe you an apology for being insensitive." She said, "Why?" I responded, "You definitely do not have to share your personal business with me, but I think the reason you haven't taken off work is that you are in a gay relationship which gives you no rights to bereavement days." That was exactly her situation.

Sometimes with dispensations of law, we can become so enmeshed in protecting our norm that we completely overlook the human needs of those who are impacted by its rigidity. My conversation with my coworker made me search myself and recognize that gay rights are here to stay. We can throw around our personal opinions and spiritual positions all day long, but the truth is that the laws of this nation now entitle same-sex couples to marriage rights. We can remain rigid, or we can accept and adapt. I have had many people ask me, "Do you think homosexuals are going to hell?" My response is consistent, "Thankfully, God has not put me on the heaven-or-hell committee. All I know is that I have a responsibility to love my neighbor." Loving my neighbor means that I have an obligation to care which means that yes, I believe Human Resource policies should grant bereavement days to same-sex couples. With each change in our society, my only ambition is to ask God to show me how to be wise. I pray Solomon's prayer from 1 Kings 3:9 and ask God to teach me how to be wise in judgments with the people. They are, after all, His people and not our own.

In our place as leaders, we must be sensitive not only to our sources of power but understand when and how to apply each.

Figure 6.3. Sources of Power

Source: Clawson, 2009

The first source of power is based on a title or position, e.g. a police officer with a badge. Coercion operates from a base of fear. "Sometimes, coercion is nothing more than force of personality, the ability to intimidate a person by fixed stares, glowers, or other facial expressions and intimations."[cxxvi] Reward offers compensation for cooperation. Expertise power is often situational and is always based on external perception of the skills level. "Finally, referent power is the ability to influence others because they admire, respect, and want to be like the leader."[cxxvii] As soon as a person says, "I want to be like (fill in the blank)," they have connected their values to someone. Whenever an interaction occurs that engages Values, Assumptions, Beliefs, and Expectations (VABE), there is a currency of reciprocity that is made available. Within the administration of law, only legitimate power and perhaps coercion have been activated.

Application

If we were interacting as consultant and client, a heavy part of my focus would center around how you and your executive team view their policies and procedures, which would include Human Resource measures. In one of my doctoral projects, I evaluated the personnel handbook for a municipal government. The document had outdated terminology (with a reference to a floppy disk) and lacked an overall professional format. It also lacked accessibility to employees as it was obviously a copy of a copy of a copy (and so on). Despite the city government having a website, there was no copy of the handbook in an electronic format. It is a worthwhile exercise to inspect the attributes and not the actual item that you want to improve. Michael Michalko (2006) has a host of brilliant activities in his book *Thinkertoys*. He offers the following blueprint for considering attributes:

1. *State your challenge.*
2. *Analyze the challenge and list as many attributes as you can.*
3. *Take each attribute, one at a time, and to try to think of ways to change or improve it.*
4. *Strive to make your thinking both fluent and flexible.*[cxxviii]

"If you tried to improve the bicycle by thinking of a bike as a whole entity, you may have left something out of consideration."[cxxix] Perhaps rather than looking at your entire set of policies, it is helpful to consider the attributes and begin a selective update process. Utilizing an inter-departmental team with a viable mix of employee, management, and executive personnel also ensures an evaluation that will prove substantial in its worth. Our best influence comes because of involvement.

In a leadership coaching session, the consideration of law is relevant to a consideration of organizational culture. The culture of an organization is revealing for both its structure and the level of cooperation it receives. Implementing Cameron and Quinn (2011) and their Competing Values Framework is a primary resource to explore the organizational culture.

Figure 6.4. Competing Values Framework

Clan (collaborative)	Adhocracy (create)
Hierarchy (control)	Market (compete)

Source: Cameron & Quinn, 2011

Across the top quadrants is the evaluation of flexibility and discretion. The lower two boxes assess stability and control. The left-side considers internal focus and integration while the right-side evaluates external focus and differentiation. Effective leadership in an organization needs to understand the purpose of its organizational structure. What best serves the vision?

With the expertise of Cameron and Quinn (2011), we can gain more detailed understanding of each culture's competencies:

Figure 6.5. Organizational Culture Competencies

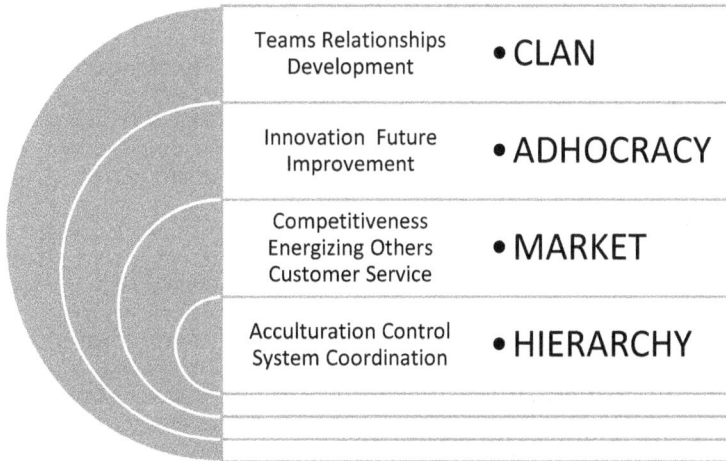

Teams Relationships Development	• CLAN
Innovation Future Improvement	• ADHOCRACY
Competitiveness Energizing Others Customer Service	• MARKET
Acculturation Control System Coordination	• HIERARCHY

Source: Cameron & Quinn, 2011

Cameron and Quinn's instruments have set global industry standards for understanding culture change from the systemic as well as the individual contributions. They generously share their expertise with multiple resources. As a consultant to an organization, their instruments are a definitive part of evaluating culture and its capacity for change.

Sidebar: The Law as King

The following insight has been on my mind for several years and is not related to any current political or judicial scenario. While considering the complex and morally chaotic world of our existence, it is ironically contradictory to the dependence on the law in the United States. The results of an internet search on the number of laws in the U.S. is a staggering, "Nobody can actually keep up with it anymore." We have become a nation of law. Guilty people dare not admit guilt and certainly cannot offer an apology as their words become the prosecution in lawsuits. The average number of Federal tort claims annually is over 512,000. Civil lawsuits cost the U.S. $239 billion dollars per year.[cxxx] We have become a nation of law. If we believe that God is God and is all-powerful and omniscient, then we also accept that He means what He says when the first of the ten commandments warns about idolatry (Exodus 20). The United States declares that we are "one nation under God" yet it is blatantly obvious that we are living a mixed message. Are we living under a judgment of law?

Ancient Israel decided that they wanted a king. God wanted them to want Him as their ruler, but they wanted a king. Finally, God (paraphrase) said, "I want you to want me, but since you want a king, go ahead. Let me know how it works out for you." It is my observation that the United States is suffering the "we want law as our king" judgment. God has said, "I want you to want me, but since you want law, go ahead. Let me know how it works out for you." We would do well to heed the words of 2 Chronicles 7:14, "If my people, which are called by my name, shall humble themselves, and pray, and seek my face, and turn from their wicked ways; then will I hear from heaven, and will forgive their sin, and will heal their land."

Reading Between the Lines

Here is a portion of a letter my mother sent to me many years ago.

Dear Kathy,

When you followed your brothers into our lives, we just assumed that you would be cuddly. Wrong! You always hated smooches, snuggling, even being held close. Where did we ever get the antiquated idea that all little girls were warm and fuzzy? You have always been an ongoing education for me. By the time you were three and had turned your doll buggy on end to catch practice balls, I admitted, "This is no ordinary little girl." At the ripe old age of one year, you tossed your bottle from the play pen proclaiming loudly, "Don't want" and you never again peacefully drank a drop of white milk. Your Dad and I watched in amazement as you outdid your brothers in everything, even things considered to be "masculine" at the time. You and I batted heads on so many issues, we were both battle scarred. Often our words were not found in any mother/daughter manual, but we kept exchanging ideas. After painful years of warfare, we met on mutual ground and look at us today.

Love, Mom

I struggled with being smart. No one pays attention to smart kids. There were times I acted as if I did not know something merely to gain interaction. I started a personal rebellion against grades. One of the nuns pulled me into the hallway, stuck her finger in my face, and said, "You have brains to burn, and you would still pass all of your classes. You could be the first female Pope if you wanted to be, and you are just belligerent!" Since I read the Reader's Digest vocabulary quizzes for entertainment, I was concerned that I had not previously heard the word belligerent. My parents would ask, "Why don't you get better grades?" My response, "I already know I'm smart, so what do I have to prove?"

Finding definition is no small undertaking. It took me decades of living to get to the painful but liberating place that I call "being reduced to God's glory." What I mean by that is being reduced to only what God knows about me as truth. One of the pieces of my puzzle that God revealed in that place is the root of my sexuality struggle. For me, it came from childhood when I saw that my brothers had options that I was not supposed to have based only on gender. I grew up wanting to be a boy, because from my perspective, boys had the power of choice. I would sometimes smear dirt on my face when we played outside because I felt empowered by the connection to being a boy.

Our society has a point of humor of talking to men about "getting in touch with their feminine side" but we have never actually made it all right for girls and women to "get in touch with their boy side." That does not have to mean that there is a divided self nor does a person have to abandon one sense of self for another. Paul wrote in Romans 8 about what the law could not do in its imperfect state. Its imperfection came from not being Spirit. He goes on to write that it is in the Spirit that we find completeness and the freedom to live without condemnation that comes in our fleshly existence. Those of us with a call to leadership deserve the internal definition that comes with spiritual influence rather than existing on external definitions that come through law.

Oh, my goodness, the wasted energy we put on trying to find definition by our own standards. Remember that no one forced Israel into Egypt. They walked in of their own volition believing that Egypt had resources they lacked. Sometimes our captivity is the result of expecting law to be our definition when God might have charted a different route through trusting Him. No wonder God had Jeremiah pen the words, "And the vessel that he made of clay was marred in the hand of the potter: so he made it again another vessel, as seemed good to the potter to make it" (Jeremiah 18:4, RSV). Even while God is working on us, other variables are present that can corrupt the original form. Thankfully, He puts us back on the wheel and keeps shaping us until we have the definition that He wants for us and that we want for ourselves.

Chapter 7

Sixth Dimension of Grace

Grace began at Calvary with the death of Jesus Christ and continues to this moment. The strength of grace is its capacity. The weakness of grace is its capacity. As the Lord originally inspired the study of dispensations, I found the dispensation of grace confusing. This is relationship number six for the woman at the well. It includes Jesus instructing her to go get her husband.

> "The woman answered him, "I have no husband." Jesus said to her, "You are right in saying, 'I have no husband'; for you have had five husbands, and he whom you now have is not your husband; this you said truly" (John 4:17-18).

Jesus called her out on her both the calculated truth she presented to him and the facts of her marital status. What does that have to do with grace? It was easy for me to relate to the woman as I started my adulthood (if you can qualify 18-years old as such) in a shack-up relationship. It was irresistible for me to ask the Lord, "What does grace have to do with a live-in relationship?" God spoke to me and said, "That is what people want in their relationship with me. They want all the privileges but not the commitment."

While my generation experienced the rebellious stance of feeling as if a marriage license was only a piece of paper, the generations that followed us have their own version of the same mistruth. It is amusing to me how the definition of fiancée has changed. It used to mean that there had been a marriage proposal and typically, an engagement ring was part of that process. In current times, it is often a label that is utilized when someone wants privileges that are attached to a commitment. For instance, I often hear the word fiancée when someone wants information they are not legally entitled to receive, e.g. medical or personal data. It is particularly challenging when the person is one the phone, and I must patiently explain, "I have to verify the information you are giving to me as I have no means through a phone call to validate your identity." The more I considered what God was showing to me about privileges and no commitment, the more it made sense to the dispensation of grace.

The Apostle Paul asks a question about grace, "What shall we say then? Are we to continue in sin that grace may abound" (Romans 6:1)? Grace is intended to cover sin, but it is not an excuse to participate in sin. Grace, privilege, and commitment are difficult variables for a conversation concerning contemporary society. From a biblical perspective, the notion of grace completely turned the rituals of Judaism inside out. Actions that necessitated sacrifice in times past now were covered by grace. Calvary was literally a world changing event. Lest we are too harsh or judgmental on those who struggled with accepting the change, take a moment to go back into Duvall and Hayes 5-step model:

Figure 7.0. Five-Step Process for Grasping Scripture

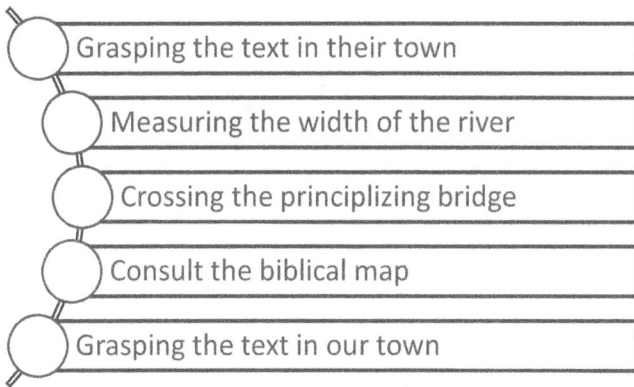

Grasping the text in their town

Measuring the width of the river

Crossing the principlizing bridge

Consult the biblical map

Grasping the text in our town

Source: Duvall & Hayes, 2012

In this case, it is a wide river to move from centuries of dedicated compliance with the standards set by God for Israel. The law contained much more than the 10 commandments. It included 613 regulations for culture and society. Jesus' ministry of grace did not devalue the culture, yet we could study this from a perspective of the upheaval of grace. Jesus provides a model of human and divine relationship that shifts from the outside-in to the inside-out. Any person who has undergone organizational change can easily move from criticism to compassion in understanding those who struggled with considering grace an upgrade from law. On the other hand, those who understood and experienced the void that law created were drawn to the message of grace. Perhaps that is why our woman at the well is a perfect character to demonstrate the filling of that void. Matthew, Mark, and Luke all document Jesus' clarification about his intended audience, "And Jesus answered them, "Those who are well have no need of a physician, but those who are sick" (Luke 5:31).

When I describe the ministry that God has given to me, I am prone to say that it is a recovery ministry. My gift is reaching for those who have struggled and those who have a history of failure. Maybe that is where you are right now. The gospel singer James Cleveland has a song with these lyrics, "Nobody told me the road would be easy, but I don't believe he brought me this far to leave me."[cxxxi] Your story does not have to be my story, but you do need to recognize that you have a story. More than that, I pray that you see that you ARE the story. One of my favorite movie scenes is from *Mary Poppins* when Mary is taking the children on a walk and comes across Burt painting on the sidewalk. With a little urging from Burt, Mary agrees to take his hand and the children's hands and suddenly, they jump INTO the painting! There is a whole new adventure waiting for them by allowing the freedom to be inside the art. When I was a child, I did not just read books, but I became part of the book. I absorbed myself into a character. Grace is a story that is meant to be told. Grace is a story that needs you to become the story.

The woman stating that she has no husband is not pertinent by her marital status. Its relevancy is that she tried to bring only a portion of her story to grace. That is why it is important that she told the people that she met someone who told her all the things she had done. It was never about her guilt. It was about her story. When we come to grace, we must bring the whole story. To leave any part of the story out is to leave that piece out from under grace. At some point, must go back and get everything that you try to leave out from under the chapters of grace. If you grasp this section of the book, the seventh dimension is an inevitable part of your story. John 1:17 tells us that grace and truth came through Jesus Christ. "The glory of the law is the glory of realizing our deficiency. It reveals our sin before a holy God. How much more glorious is the grace of God which tells us we have a remedy for our problem! Grace and truth came through Jesus Christ."[cxxxii] Mercy shows up whether we are a believer or not, but grace is a mindful connection to accepting what the presence of Christ will do in us. Grace is the result of the action of believing. Charles Spurgeon offers this view of grace, "The general call of the gospel is like the common 'cluck' of the hen which she is always giving when her chickens are around her. But if there is any danger impending, then she gives a very peculiar call, quite different from the ordinary one, and the little chicks come running as fast as they can, and hide for safety under her wings."[cxxxiii]

Another one of the fathers of the New Testament church is R.C. Sproul. As he describes grace, it is placed in economic terminology. We have a debt that is impossible to be paid by our own efforts. Jesus Christ freely provides grace that has the capacity of clearing our debt.

"Grace should never cease to amaze us. God has an absolute, pure, holy standard of justice. That's why we cling with all our might to the merit of Jesus Christ. He alone has the merit to satisfy the demands of God's justice, and He gives it freely to us. We haven't merited it. There's nothing in us that elicits the Lord's favor that leads to our justification. It's pure grace."[cxxxiv]

Grace is a story demanding to be told. It is the sixth dimension of relationship for the woman. It is the relationship where culture says she did not marry because she had no more dowry. She was broken and broke. She could not resolve the need for a relationship out of tradition or culture. The man who chose to be in a relationship with her represents grace. It was not profitable for him to take on a relationship with her. He gained nothing from it. The same way that this unknown man took a step down on the social ladder to take the hand of a woman he loved, so Jesus stepped down from glory to take our hand in grace.

May I take a slight detour to speak to those who struggle with accepting any sort of spiritual teaching over a scientific paradigm? Perhaps there is room in scientific thinking to accommodate spirituality as a complement and not a contradiction.

"Sin is what lures and tempts people to place science outside of a relationship with God, thereby stealing science from God, and ultimately turning science against God."[cxxxv] Kuyper's call is equally beneficial to the believer who has been persuaded to minimize scholarly disciplines as if they diminish spiritual processes. Creation is an extension of God; therefore, science can be categorized as a spiritual discipline. Kuyper teaches that sin darkens the knowledge of science by making it a secular field of study while grace illuminates the sciences to a reconnection with their originator – Creator God. How is this relevant to our woman at the well? Science is engaged in her story as it centers on the nature of water. Of God's creation, it is only the human being who has been given the capability of understanding the presence of God in our surroundings. Jesus needed the woman to understand grace, and He accomplished that by using what was present and natural – water.

Please recall our earlier admonition that nothing is coincidental when we are dealing with the divine. There are nearly 400 mentions of water in the scripture, beginning with creation. Adding the plural form of water adds nearly another 300 mentions. "And the earth was without form, and void; and darkness was upon the face of the deep. And the Spirit of God moved upon the face of the waters" (Genesis 1:2). By adding sea, seas, rivers, and wells, our count goes up by another 1,000 plus citations. The scriptural saga opens and closes with the presence of a river. "And a river went out of Eden to water the garden; and from thence it was parted, and became into four heads" (Genesis 2:10). "And he shewed me a pure river of water of life, clear as crystal, proceeding out of the throne of God and of the Lamb" (Revelation 22:1). Here is a summary of the presence of water in the gospels:

Figure 7.1. Water in the Gospels

GOSPEL	CONTEXT
Matthew 3:11	John the Baptist stating that he baptizes with water.
Matthew 3:16	Jesus is baptized.
Matthew 14:28	Peter walks on water to meet Jesus.
Matthew 17:15	Demon-possessed boy falls into water and fire.
Matthew 17:24	Pilate washes his hands with water as disclaimer to Jesus' fate
Luke 8:23	The ship carrying the disciples and Jesus is filled with water in a storm.
Luke 16:24	The Rich man asks if Lazarus can dip his finger in water to cool his tongue.
John 2:7	Wedding at Cana – Jesus instructs water pots to be filled.
John 4:7	8 mentions of water in the story of the woman at the well.
John 5:3	Story of lame man at Pool of Bethesda

John 7:38	He that believeth on me, as the scripture hath said, out of his belly shall flow rivers of living water.
John 13:5	Jesus washes the disciples' feet with water.
John 19:34	But one of the soldiers with a spear pierced his side, and forthwith came there out blood and water.

Source: Williams, 2016

When we are born, our bodies are nearly 80 percent water. As adults, we are still composed of approximately 60 percent water. "Earth is known as the "Blue Planet" because 71 percent of the Earth's surface is covered with water."[cxxxvi] Jesus could have interacted with the woman over any number of items or events, but He chose to interact with her over water. The human longing for God is symbolized by water.

> "In Jewish-Christian cosmology, water is a fundamental element of creation (Genesis 1, 6-9). Further, in the biblical tradition, control of the waters, the forces of primeval chaos, is the prerogative of God alone (Job 9:8, 38:16; Psalm 77:20; Habakkuk 3:15; Isaiah 51:9-10). In the Gospel of John, Jesus' power over the waters identifies him with God and the water imagery in his teaching affirms the provocative nature of his messianic mission."[cxxxvii]

Because water also symbolizes cleansing and healing, Jesus offered the woman something that no other dispensation could offer – to cover the disappointments of innocence, conscience, authority, promise, and law. Grace comes with a capacity to cleanse and heal the past, create a purpose for the present, and set an ambition for the future.

Someone might say, "Wait a minute. He talked to her about worship and spirit and truth." Yes, that is true, but ultimately, He wanted her to know that the Messiah was right in front of her. The Messiah was equivalent to a divine prince. What does royalty have the power to do but to condemn or assign life? That is grace. Grace assigns life when death is deserved. One of my repeated statements to the men who are incarcerated is this, "When you realize that the State of Indiana did not **put** you here, but God **sent** you here, then you must ask Him what you are supposed to do with your time?" Grace makes sense of why we are where we are when we are there. Grace is closely connected to timing and placement. For many years, I wanted to have a radio talk show. Just think of the mess I would have made of other people's lives if I had stretched into that ministry when I thought I was ready for it. You see, after I thought that is what God wanted me to do, I became so distressed that I walked out on my life. I left the church and ministry and tried my best to persuade God to leave me alone. I did not want my calling. I wanted to be "normal" and not face all the turmoil that comes with ministry and leadership. Thankfully, I can testify today that my season of running away was nearly 20 years ago. The change came when I made a commitment, "God, I promise you from this day forward I will live by faith. If you don't bring it into my life, I don't need it or want it." When moments of struggle came, I learned to pray, "God, teach me how to let you be enough in this situation." I learned to put my whole story under grace.

Grace came to our woman at the well when she began to understand the connection between what she knew and the man that was conversing with her. "Audiences might remember that Hosea, the prophet to the northern kingdom, primarily used the language of marriage, and broken marriage, to speak of the northern kingdom's covenant relationship with God and what he considered its breach of that covenant. Thus, Jesus is also articulating the current broken state of the Samaritans' relationship. The woman gleans this and begins to see Jesus is a prophet. This, for her as a Samaritan, opens the discussion to the possibility of Christology."[cxxxviii] It has been my experience that most Muslims own both a Holy Qur'an and a Holy Bible. Many men that I have met through the Chapel who participate in non-Christian religions have some experience with Christianity, whether going to church as a child or some other encounter. What we, as Christians have failed to do is operate in any sort of reciprocity. Once again, the exchange is not with the agenda of lessening our Christian self but for the advantage of having a well-informed global self. Unfortunately, many are of other faiths because of discouragement from within the Christian church. I am a stickler about how Christians conduct themselves, including the most basic of good manners. We never know that we may be the first Christian someone encounters, and what is their impression of us from that encounter? One encounter above others stands out to me. When a volunteer ministry must cancel their scheduled service, my first prayer is, "God, what do you want to do this evening?"

On the night of one of those cancellations, I knew that I was supposed to ask eight men to take one each of the beatitudes. One by one, my request for a man to take one of the beatitudes was complete. I also knew that Matthew 5:8, "Blessed *are* the pure in heart: for they shall see God" was to be assigned to a young man. The Lord directed me to a young gay man who was extraordinarily flamboyant with a walk deserving of *America's Next Top Model*.

His walk literally turned heads when he came into the room as his graceful (appropriate word) movements were professionally eloquent. When I asked him to be the speaker for Matthew 5:8, he admitted that he did not own a Bible. I said, "That's all right. I can get one for you." He then admitted that he had never read Matthew. I said, "That's all right. I will help you." He said, "Chaplain, I don't know. I don't like being in front of people." I assured him that he would be fine, and I would be within view to encourage him. After man after man spoke, it was the young man's turn. He got up and softly said, "Chaplain Williams asked me to speak, and I didn't think I had anything to say." Suddenly his voice got stronger and with a bit of a snap, he said, "But I think I do have something I want to say." He went on to say that he had never gone to church before coming to prison. He said that he didn't bother going to church when he was a kid because he knew he was gay and he knew the church people would tell him he was going to hell. He said he came to the Chapel just to have something to do. Then he said, "But when I got here, Chaplain Williams welcomed me, and you welcomed me, and for the first time in my life, I have a church." I sat with tears running down my face. When he finished, I broke all the rules and gave him a big hug. The whole Chapel gave him a standing ovation for his testimony. With the woman at the well, Jesus role modeled the most basic example of grace – accept people for who they are and where they are at that moment. If we do not step into the present of people's lives, we lose the privilege of respectfully participating in where they are going.

Application

This application section is crucial for contemporary leadership. Let's focus on the woman at the well bringing her whole story to the experience. It is impossible to effectively function in our 21st-century world and not have tools for the cross-cultural interface. That last statement has some reservation about it as people have the option of constructing the world that suits their view and consciously not having any outsiders welcome, but is that the world that most of us want? The answer is probably not. This section is offered believing that readers want interaction. Here is a summary of nine essential competencies to three domains of cross-cultural agility[cxxxix]:

Figure 7.2. Competencies to Cross-Cultural Agility

Competencies Affecting Psychological Ease	
Competency	**Explanation**
Tolerance of Ambiguity	Level of comfort in an unfamiliar setting.
Appropriate Self-Efficacy	Balanced by humility – knowing abilities in cross-cultural settings.
Cultural Curiosity and Desire to Learn	Interest in other cultures and pursuit of learning.
Competencies Affecting Cross-Cultural Interactions	
Valuing Diversity	Comfort level in being around others not like yourself.
Ability to Form Relationships	Interest in personal connections to others not like you.
Perspective-Taking	*An ability to see situations from multiple perspectives and reassign meaning to those behaviors.*
Cross-Cultural Competencies Affecting Decisions	

Knowledge and Integration of Cross-Cultural or National Issues	Factual knowledge and understanding of global interconnections.
Receptivity to Adopting Diverse Ideas	*The interest in exploring diverse solutions and willingness to adopt solutions, approaches, or practices that originate from atypical sources.*
Divergent Thinking and Creativity	Having multiple ideas and generating multiple solutions through the skills of resourcefulness, innovation, and creativity.

Source: Caligiuri, 2012

Jesus interaction with the woman is a classic scenario to study cross-cultural agility. Their conversation contains multiple points where He could have put his energy on trying to change or convert her to His way of thinking. He could have criticized her, or frankly, He could have ignored her. Remember that Jesus changed water into wine, and fed thousands with a few pieces of fish and loaves of bread. He could have met His own need for water. Perhaps the groundwork for grace was laid back in the wilderness when the Tempter (KJV) showed up at the moment of Jesus' hunger to tempt Jesus to simply turn stones to bread. The Message version of Matthew 4:4 gives Jesus response as, ""It takes more than bread to stay alive. It takes a steady stream of words from God's mouth." Jesus knew that interacting with the woman was more important than gaining a drink of water. He did not just converse with her; He initiated a flow of conversation that used her culture as a basis.

To become effective cross-culturally, we must be willing to dig deeply into our motivations. Why do we want what we want for others? Is it because it will better their lives or because it will bring ease to our own? As leaders, we must constantly push at our motives to be sure that we have the best interests of others in place. If we consider Return on Investment (ROI), we see that Jesus used one woman and gained the major portion of a town as followers. It is a viable practice to utilize assessment tools for your leadership team and at every level of the organization that requires cross-cultural skills. The step beyond assessment is learning, and, more importantly, creating a learning experience that builds trust. "One of the distortions that we as human beings bring to social relationships is that of making our familiar structure the only structure that God can use to accomplish his purpose."[cxl] Can God use the Native American Grandfather teachings for us to expound on our beliefs as Christians? The answer is affirmative. Can Jesus accomplish ministry by listening to the woman talk about the differences between Samaritans and Jews? Clearly, He did. "By denying the validity of other structures, we force people to submit to our standards and structures of relationship in order to accomplish the work and purpose of God."[cxli] We must master not only listening but hearing others.

Each year, Muslims participate in Ramadan. It is a fast lasting for 30 days. It recognizes the time that Allah revealed the Holy Qur'an to the Prophet Muhammad. Muslims eat a meal before the breaking of the day and another after the setting of the sun. There is no food or water consumed between those two meals. "The Quran tells us that fasting is prescribed for you so that you may fear God (Al-Baqarah, 2: 183). So, what does it mean to fear God? Fearing God means that man should acknowledge his helplessness vis-à-vis God's greatness."[cxlii] Muslims who are incarcerated have a right to have Ramadan supported by meals served at appropriate times. The Chapel coordinates the schedule with the kitchen. A few years ago, the meal service in the morning ran late which forces the Muslims to not eat until night. After 3 days of hearing complaints, I went to work at 4:00 am so that I could ensure the meal delivery was happening by 4:30 am. I spoke with the kitchen workers and went to my office to complete a report for my supervisor. When he went to the executive team meeting at 8:00 am and presented the problem, the kitchen supervisor challenged the information. "How do you know this to be true?" Thankfully my supervisor could say, "One of my chaplains was in the kitchen at 4:00 am to personally confirm the delivery (or not) of breakfast." My reason for sharing is not to give myself a pat on the back but to arrive at the next step. In a meeting with my supervisor, I proposed a religious workshop for the kitchen staff. Did they understand Ramadan? Do they understand the Catholic's Lent? Has anyone taken the time to educate them about the importance of timing when it comes to certain fasts? We cannot be upset with people who we have not educated. Lingenfelter (2008) poses an ideal called *power-giving leadership*. "Power-giving leadership is in its essence relational, rather than positional."[cxliii] Authority and control become secondary to the value of people. Administrators could have given the kitchen workers orders that likely would have been carried out but how much better to empower the staff with knowledge.

Take time to invest in your team such that they have clarity concerning divergence and convergence.

Figure 7.3. Convergence or Divergence

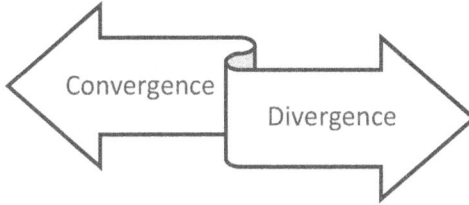

Source: Williams, 2016

"Tapping divergence refers to value that takes advantage of differing skills, resources, and demand patterns present in various parts of the world. Tapping convergence, in contrast, refers to commonalities, to the needs and resources that people have everywhere."[cxliv] Jesus masterfully uses both in the encounter with the Samaritan woman. Perhaps the disciples became unwitting students to the lesson of cultural agility when they returned to find Jesus in conversation with someone they would not have engaged. Remember that in the not-too-distant future, they will be the recipients of an instruction to go and teach all nations (Matthew 28:19). Never underestimate the small encounters with diversity. Those brief encounters could be setting the stage for the bigger picture of your destiny. "The danger to all leaders is that they will become comfortable in their practices. It's entirely possible that a once-cultivated global mind will begin relying on stereotypes and simplifications."[cxlv]

In the prison where I am a chaplain, there are approximately 150 Hispanic inmates that represent up to 8 different Hispanic nations, including Guatemala, Mexico, Venezuela, Spain, Puerto Rico, the Dominican Republic and others. In Mexico, a *chabacano* is an apricot. In Spain, a *chabacano* is a vulgar person. In Chile, a *guagua* is a baby. In Puerto Rico, it is a bus. Currently, two of our clerks are Hispanic. One speaks limited English, and I speak minimal Spanish. We are quite a hilarious combination on some days. Nevertheless, we wade through our conversations. We had a Russian inmate a few years ago. He rarely wore his coat in the winter and scoffed at what Indiana believes the word "cold" means. One of the more challenging requests was to locate a Bible written in Burmese as one of our inmates could read only in his native language. It is fair to say that many of us are now accustomed to gas stations where the owners or managers are from the Middle East. They speak English to the customer, but their conversations with one another are in their own tongue. How much effort do we make to expose ourselves to cross-cultural settings? It no longer requires a passport or an airline ticket. Most of us can find it within our city. How much diversity is within your organization?

How does your organization support diversity? Do you have a newsletter that could note Ramadan or Cinco de Mayo or other cultural holidays? Does your organization host multicultural events? If you are a pastor, does your leadership team have an active plan for developing a diverse congregation? Do you have a burden for diversity, or is it something that you tolerate? Does your organization meet compliance standards and consider that an accomplishment? Culturally diversity does not necessarily mean a different language. During a mission trip to Jamaica, our team spent the day at the village market. Jamaican English and Indiana English is virtually two different languages. I bravely went into a local bakery to buy some bulla bread. Bulla bread is a wonderful, sweet soft bread. To this day, I have no idea what I said, but the baker handed me a big flat loaf of black bread. When I tried to explain that it was not what I wanted, she shooed me out of her store with animated gestures and clearly a verbal disdain for my American incompetence. I also had received no change for my Jamaican currency. As I turned to leave, our host pastor came in the door with gestures and language equal to the baker. All I know is that I left with some bulla bread and my change.

Use the dimension of grace to allow others to bring their story. Shifting away from our comfort zone is never an easy task, so make it an entertaining opportunity. Host international cuisine days as a pitch-in effort. Use creative programs to ease your team into developing cultural agility. Promote a 360-degree perspective. I strongly encourage you to invest in a copy (or copies) of Michael Michalko's (2009) *Thinkertoys, 2nd edition* as a resource for creative thinking development. For example, the Lotus Blossom is an exercise that fits cultural agility:

> "You start with a problem or idea and expand that theme into themes until you've created several different entry points. In the Lotus Blossom, the petals, or themes, around the core of the blossom are figuratively peeled back one at a time, revealing a key component or sub-theme."[cxlvi]

Creative thinking is a form of professional play time, and it is a worthwhile investment. "Directed imagination focuses you on how to solve a problem instead of wondering if the problem can be solved."[cxlvii] One of the greatest pieces of advice I have ever received happened around 30 years ago. Someone asked me to do something, and I responded, "I can't." The person said, "Never say 'I can't' but say 'I haven't learned yet.' That changed my life in how I approached something I had not done before. When we let go of "I can't," we open ourselves to a lifetime of learning potential.

Reading Between the Lines

Before we delve into the seventh dimension, I have another experiential lesson to consider. Our body has systems that are considered autonomic. We do not have to think to breathe or to have our heart beat or to blink our eyes. In His creative perfection, God set systems in place that need no assistance from us. In a sense, Adam and Eve had the perfect spiritual autonomic environment prior to eating from the forbidden tree.

On one of my worse days as an addict, I had spent the day with my boyfriend drinking various kinds of liquor, smoking pot, snorting coke (cocaine), and shooting speed (intravenous injections). We went to Indianapolis to do a drug pick-up from a locker at the bus station. As we drove west on 38th Street, I saw a man flying beside the car. He told me to open the door and come and fly with him. I was afraid of my boyfriend and told the man (all of this in my mind and not actual) that I could not fly with him as I would get into trouble. He kept insisting that I had the power

*to fly. I started to move my hand toward the doorknob. When I
moved my hand, I could see (or so I thought) the blood flowing
through the veins through my translucent skin. I could also see my
heart beating and watched my lungs working. I could see through
my own body. I became so engaged in what my body was doing
that I started to get involved with my breathing and my heart
beating. Because I was consciously interfering with autonomic
functions, it was like throwing a screwdriver into the cogs of a
wheel. My overdose became more and more apparent with every
interference that I caused in those systems. My boyfriend saw
what was happening and asked if I wanted to go to the hospital. I
was more afraid of being arrested than of dying, and I insisted I
was all right. The drug dealer that was riding with us told him to
get me to drink some orange juice to break the high. Who knows?*

     *Why tell such a morbid story? I told that story to provoke
us to consider that outside of operating in sovereign reign,
anything else we do is merely an interference with spiritual
autonomic systems. God had a plan. Humanity tried to better that
plan with their own will. With each successive dispensation, we
have only worsened the overdose of our human meddling. When
we get to seventh dimension leadership, we have the wonderful
opportunity to take ourselves out of the picture (or should I say our*

"self") and let God oversee the plan once again. Jesus told us again and again that His presence in the earth was directed by the will of the Father. Stepping into the seventh dimension is embracing the will of the Father.

Chapter 8

Seventh Dimension of Sovereign Reign

For most dispensationalists, sovereign reign begins when Jesus comes back to the earth and ends in the conclusion of the Book of Revelation. The strength of sovereign reign is its everlasting presence. There is no weakness in this dispensation. It is the author's premise that sovereign reign does not have to begin at the second coming but is activated by our alignment to the sovereignty of Christ. Luke's gospel records the disciples asking Jesus to teach them to pray. A significant part of the model Jesus presented includes the words, "thy will be done as in heaven, so in earth" (Luke 11:2). Jesus repeatedly expressed that He was on earth to do the will of the Father. A fascinating declaration takes place at His trial when Pilate asked Jesus if He understood that Pilate held the power to crucify or to release. Jesus responded, "You would have no power over me unless it had been given you from above . . ." (John 19:11). Once again, without the Father's permission, not even our enemies have any power. The authority or power that is spoken of here is judiciary power. It might seem that the crucifixion contradicts Jesus' declaration, but let us take another look. Jesus was not subjected to the cross. He is the subject of the cross. "And being found in human form he humbled himself and became obedient unto death, even death on a cross" (Philippians 2:8, RSV). The *kingdom of God* is used in the New Testament 68 times, and the *kingdom of heaven* is used 31 times. Every kingdom has a sovereign ruler. In Christianity, that king is Jesus Christ. It is more than recitation to believe that the path to salvation is Romans 10:9, ". . . if you confess with your lips that Jesus is Lord and believe in your heart that God raised him from the dead, you will be saved." To say that Jesus is Lord is saying that He is sovereign. In a monarchy, the king has the ultimate power. While there might be advisors and close comrades, a king is subject to no other authority. Our king went to the cross to cleanse us and to set an example for righteousness, "And he said to all, "If any man would come after me, let him deny himself and take up his cross daily and follow me" (Luke 9:23). Sovereign reign requires a decisive course of action.

Let's insert the conclusion of the matter, and then we will explore the details. While the seventh dispensation is constructed around the return of Jesus to the earth, we do not have to wait for an event to allow Him to have sovereign reign. Through the Holy Spirit, we have access to His presence as king right now. Jesus told us four times that He was going to send a Comforter and offered the assurance that we would have the Comforter forever. In John 14:26, Jesus specifically relates that the Comforter is the Holy Ghost. One of the reasons for the presence of the Spirit is that there is a capacity given to be a student of the Spirit in that, ". . . He will teach you all things . . .." The didactic nature of our relationship with the Spirit is to be a lifelong learner of kingdom lessons. Clearly, Jesus did not leave that outcome to a point beyond a timeline in the earth realm. We are given the indwelling of the Spirit to empower us here and now. While the term is sadly as overused as the concept of a product advertised as *artisan,* please allow me the grace to use the term *paradigm.* Kuhn (2012) said, "Probably the single most prevalent claim advanced by the proponents of a new paradigm is that they can solve the problems that have led the old one to crisis."[cxlviii] Jesus assures us that the empowerment He represents does not eliminate but completes what the Jewish culture has known.

Our main character, the woman at the well, is a dynamic example of exactly what Jesus intends with the spiritual empowerment. At the time of meeting Him, she has had five husbands and is presently in a relationship with someone outside of marriage. After six natural relationships, she steps into a supernatural relationship with Jesus Christ. Many of us can relate to being the person no one else thought would qualify for leadership. Our past is immediate proof of why our name should be eliminated from consideration. There are many times when I have said to an inmate, "Believe me, I am the most fascinated of all that I am sitting here as a chaplain." As a young person, I sincerely believed that I was meant to go to hell. I used Judas as my evidence to prove my point. Many times, I have told the men in the prison that the key to changing their mindset is to shift from fact to truth. The fact is that they are a convicted felon. The truth is that whom the Son has set free is free indeed (John 8:36). The fact is that many of them will be on the sex offender registry. The truth is, "Nay, in all these things, we are more than conquerors through him that loved us" (Romans 8:37). We are not conquerors on our own; the disclaimer is that our overcoming is takes place *through* Jesus. Philippians 4:13 declares that I can do all things *through* Christ. The primary preposition from the Romans writing refers to the channel of an action while the preposition used in Philippians is much more interesting.

The preposition *en* in Philippians 4:13 has the following etymology, "A primary preposition denoting (fixed) position (in place, time or state), and (by implication) instrumentality (medially or constructively)."[cxlix] Thayer's Greek Lexicon broadens the preposition to mean *in the interior of some whole*.[cl] In recent years, there has been a movement called WWJD which means What Would Jesus Do? The movement is intended to provoke people to stop and consider what Jesus would do in a certain situation and align their actions to the supposed outcome. Thankfully, the scripture does not leave us with that lingering question. The scripture provides direction and strategy. Many Christians think of salvation as an act of letting Jesus into our lives. More so, many consider the filling of the Holy Spirit to be the presence of God inside of us. What if we are selling ourselves short with that perception? What if the more powerful position is for us to be inside of Jesus? Dare we suggest that God is the subject, and we are the object?

> "The Hebrew scriptures try to show this intimacy in a God who laughs and weeps, a God whose glory is a word implying weight, or, better, density. And this very glory is kenotic: God is willing to be given over in Name; to participate in history; to dwell between the cherubim of the Ark; to become an infant; to laugh and weep and to be crucified. God's *kenosis* is God's potency."[cli]

Do you remember my love of watching airplanes overhead? It is only when we are inside the power of the plane that it moves us from point to point. I cannot put the plane inside of me; I must have a ticket to enter its existence. Perhaps sovereign reign is not about us possessing salvation or power but of allowing our Sovereign King to have possession of us.

For many, we have attempted to own the glory of God by boxing it into our denominational systems. What did God want us to do with His presence? Were we supposed to close ourselves into a building on Sunday? I am not, in any way, discouraging denominational membership or church attendance. We all need the fellowship of like-minded believers. The caution is to not confuse church with Christianity as our commitment is much broader in scope. We spend a great deal of time determining who deserves heaven and who should suffer hell, but the words of Jesus offer some clarity on what He found to among our responsibilities. Matthew 25:31-46 outlines a specific list of ministry tasks that Jesus will use to separate those who will receive eternal life and those who will deserve damnation. Here is a breakdown of our "to do" list:

Figure 8.0. Ministry "To Do" List

SCRIPTURE	CONDITION	RESPONSE
Matthew 25:35	Hunger	Give food
Matthew 25:35	Thirsty	Give drink
Matthew 25:35	Stranger	Welcoming
Matthew 25:36	Naked	Give clothing
Matthew 25:36	Sick	Visit
Matthew 25:36	Imprisoned	Come see

Source: Williams, 2016

May I share with you that the number one reason we have
difficulties getting ministries to come to the prison on Wednesday
evening is this, "That is the night of our Bible Study." Do you see
the problem with that logic that I do? I am not judging or
criticizing. I need to work on the assignment of visiting the sick
(among many others). For years, I have said that I am going to the
local hospital and complete volunteer training to hold newborns,
especially those born with addictions. I was curious as to why

Jesus told them to visit the sick but to come see those in prison. The concept of *visit* is relative to examining the person with your eyes while the concept of *come see* refers to becoming known to the person. It speaks to an established connection. The stipulation that Jesus set is that the actions he wants from us are to be directed to strangers. In the case of those who complied and those who did not, they had the same question, "Lord, when did we see thee hungry and feed thee, or thirsty and give thee drink" (Matthew 25:37, RSV)? We also have the consideration of cultural differences. In the U.S., we are accustomed to systems taking care of the Matthew 25 obligations. One of the striking differences is that in many other nations, if a loved one must be hospitalized, it is the family's responsibility to provide sheets and blankets and bring meals.

In sovereign reign, one of the drivers for your organization is corporate social responsibility. For a small, local business, it may be sponsoring a Little League team. The larger the organization, the broader the scope of activity can become. Organizational participation exponentially increases Jesus' scope of hunger, thirst, disconnection, nakedness, sickness, and imprisonment to historic levels. My signature line for many years is a quote of Anne Frank, WWII concentration camp survivor,

"How wonderful it is that nobody need wait a single moment to improve the world." We do not have to become trapped by the cynicism or pessimism of others. In sovereign reign, we are liberated to doing good for the sake of doing good. Paul told the Galatians, "And let us not be weary in well doing: for in due season we shall reap, if we faint not" (Galatians 6:9). Take heart that there are 103 verses of scripture that support do-gooders by telling us to "do good." The balance that is needed in sovereign reign is found in the intention. Jesus tells us over and over that He is there to glorify the Father and not to take credit for himself. That mindset will shelter you from the disappointment guaranteed to come when we look to others for gratification. Our greatest joy is that we did it with a kingdom mindset that glorifies God. "Whatever your task, work heartily, as serving the Lord and not men" (Colossians 3:23).

Many are bothered by the notion that the Bible quotes Jesus telling us to be perfect (Matthew 5:48). Listen to the voice of C.S. Lewis on that point,

> "Some people seem to think that this means 'Unless you are perfect, I will not help you' and as we cannot be perfect, then if He meant that, our position is hopeless. I think He meant, 'The

only help I will give is help you to become perfect. You may want something less, but I will give you nothing less."[clii]

Does that mean there will be no more struggle? That would be a fantasy world that can only happen in a video game (with frequent use of the reset button). Jesus made His statement to Pilate, and then He went to the cross. Sovereign reign does not take away struggle. It gives the struggle definition. One of the most prevalent biblical characters that demonstrate struggle is the Apostle Peter. He is a fascinating character who demonstrates all the very human characteristics of someone striving to find their destiny. Can you imagine holding one career all your life only to find out that you were sort of on the right path but missed the application? Peter's upbringing was a fisherman. It was a family business. Yet, when Jesus came along, Peter experienced a pivot. He had understood the fishing part of his destiny correctly, but Jesus let Peter know that he would no longer fish for fish but would become a fisher of men. In fact, Jesus graciously allowed Peter and Andrew to remain together which kept the family business aspect of their fishing career intact. He changed their product line but made use of their experience. The business world would consider this a moment of disruptive innovation.

Mark 9:2-13 relates a marvelous story and a significant insight into the man who would become the Catholic Church's first pope. Peter was one of three who was in the inner circle among Jesus' disciples. He was a chief part of the succession plan for Jesus' ministry. In fact, it can be suggested that Jesus kept His word that He had not come to destroy the law or prophets but to fulfill them (Matthew 5:17). The concept of destroying that Jesus used references overthrowing a system or halting a journey. The order of civilization began in a tribal form based on family identity. Jesus made it clear that family meant those who do the will of the Father. They are His mother and brother and sister (Matthew 12:50). "In all organization, both tacit and explicit knowledge is a necessity to succeed, depending on the type of organization. However, in family business, the balance leans significantly towards tacit knowledge."[cliii] With the description of the New Testament church in Acts 17:6 as, ". . . these that have turned the world upside down . . .." we know that the experiential factor continued to strengthen. However, passing the baton of leadership is not a simple task.

In the world of track running, passing the baton must be practiced again and again. Coaches say that the key is timing, but it is about much more than pacing and speed. "Building trust and chemistry is key to this drill . . . ."[cliv] It is easy to look at Peter (or other leaders) and see the multiple points where he seems to boggle the task at hand. He is the one who denied Jesus, not once but three times. In one incident, Jesus called him Satan. My favorite scene where Peter seems at a loss is an event most call the Mount of Transfiguration. Peter is standing with Jesus who was transfigured until the Bible says, "And his raiment became shining, exceeding white as snow; so as no fuller on earth can white them" (Mark 9:3, KJV). If that wasn't enough, Moses and Elijah showed up! Peter speaks up and offers to build tents for each Jesus, Moses, and Elijah. His reasoning for making the offer is very human. "For he wist not what to say . . ." (Mark 9:6). The Message version of scripture states it more plainly, "He blurted this out without thinking, stunned as they all were by what they were seeing."

There is a reason that I am taking so much time with the narrative of Peter and the ups and downs of his career development. Realistically, our ups and our downs are not always separate events. We can have them simultaneously, but the all or nothing thinking of traditional leadership models would insinuate that it must be one or the other. It was stated much earlier in this writing that the goal of leadership is not perfection, but it must include maturity and development. I learned a life lesson standing on top of Mt. Mansfield in Stowe, Vermont. A friend of mine had brain cancer and wanted to make a trip to the East Coast. She had property in Vermont and asked if I wanted to be her driver. I was on welfare at the time and living in a cockroach infested apartment in a ghetto neighborhood dominated by the Black Gangster Disciples. Traveling and vacations were not part of my lifestyle. It was, in fact, the first time in my life that I had seen mountains or the ocean (we also went to Maine). As we started the hike up the mountain's trail, my instructions from my friend had been simple, "Follow me, and don't look down." At the top of the mountain, all I could do was stand in amazement with tears running down my face and say, "Look how big God is!" That is when I learned the lesson. I stepped off the path to get a closer look over the edge. There was a teacher with a group of students, and one of the children also stepped off the path. The teacher said, "Stay on the path because the growth at the top of the mountain is tender and easily destroyed."

Literature often paints a picture of victory when speaking of a mountaintop experience, but the teacher offered a life-changing perspective. The growth we have in our moments of success is tender and easily destroyed (or disrupted). Even though

Peter was having an incredulous experience, he was also unsure of himself and is recorded as simply not knowing what to say or do. With some a humorous side note, Peter was a fisherman offering to build tents. How many of us have ever been in a situation that we simply blundered our way through? Even when we are at the top, there is more to learn. The seventh dimension of sovereign reign does not mean the journey is complete. Remember the words of my mentor, "None of us have arrived, because the minute you think you did, you didn't." The Chinese characters for the word learning mean both *to study* and *to practice constantly.*[clv] Jesus relationship to Peter is a classic example of competency development, particularly in light of succession planning. "I will give you the keys of the kingdom of heaven, and whatever you bind on earth shall be bound in heaven, and whatever you loose on earth shall be loosed in heaven" (Matthew 16:19). While Peter was given the declaration of succession in the middle of Matthew's gospel, we know that he did not fully accept that role until the Book of Acts. Peter is well able to close his epistle with this admonition of growth, "But grow in the grace and knowledge of our Lord and Savior Jesus Christ. To him be the glory both now and to the day of eternity. Amen" (1 Peter 3:18).

One of the major concepts that Jesus brought to religion is the way that it is interpreted and the core practices of those who participate. In our contemporary world, He would be an extraordinary leader for a learning organization. ". . . the primary leverage for any organizational learning effort lies not in policies, budgets, or organizational charts, but in ourselves."[clvi] When Jesus said that He did not come to destroy the law or prophets but to fulfill, He was saying that His mission was not to change the structure of spirituality but to change what Senge, et. al. (1994) calls, ". . . the hard-to-see patterns of interaction between people and processes."[clvii] Sovereign reign grows beyond cultural, ethnic, gender, and other societally imposed differences. It extends beyond historical roots (John 4:20), tradition, and folklore. Sovereign reign engages spirit and truth. It is when Jesus convinced the woman at the well to understand who she was that there was a permanent shift in her capacity for the spiritual. She had a metamorphic experience of working alone at a well to serving as the voice for change in an entire community. Embracing the future into her present was the catalyst.

Sometimes, one conversation can change us forever. What if you had a journal of those moments and used it as a reference tool? One of those moments came for me in a conversation with another chaplain. We were discussing a guideline that had been implemented for our department. I casually made the comment, "I told them that five years ago, but you already know that nobody listens to me." I followed that with, "My goddaughter tells me again and again that I live ahead of my time so nobody really knows what I am talking about anyway." He said, "Isn't that what it means to be prophetic?" I responded, "Yes, I supposed it is. Being prophetic means pulling the future into the present." His next statement gave me one of those "forever and ever" moments, "For you, it never was the future." Our role as leaders in the 21st century is unavoidably tied to our ability to become strategic futurists. "Understanding and preparing for the future – and learning to use the tools that make it possible – is a responsibility all of us share . . . Everyone needs to think differently about the future, a future that is riddled with change, challenge, and risk."[clviii]

John's narrative concerning the woman at the well is not concluded until John 4:42 when the people of the city testify that their conversion is no longer based on the woman's testimony but on their own belief. "They said to the woman, "It is no longer because of your words that we believe, for we have heard for ourselves, and we know that this is indeed the Savior of the world" (John 4:42, RSV). Pfeffer and Sutton (2000) addressed a challenge called *the knowing-doing gap*, ". . . the challenge of turning knowledge about how to enhance organizational performance into actions consistent with that knowledge."[clix] One of my greatest strengths in leadership and in ministry is that I am a storyteller. I narrate life. I have said many times that if God would have let me be anything I wanted to be, I would be an African griot. A griot explains the unexplainable by telling stories about it. Like the woman at the well, my personal story is filled with a long series of failures, struggles, and pain. It is absurd to believe that the woman telling others that Jesus saw through her façade was enough to convert a whole city. The people she talked to already knew her story. Her story is not what brought them to a place of listening differently to the man who might very well be the Messiah. Her testimony of finding purpose in her story is what drew their interest.

Tavis Smiley wrote a book titled *Fail Up* (2011). One of this chapters is titled "Save Space for Grace." Mr. Smiley, known for his liberal political commentating and a host for PBS, uses the book to share the story of his career with a focus on his failures. He tells a story about an interview on BET when a famous guest didn't seem to know that Egypt is in Africa. His first instinct was to expose the person's ignorance and get the upper hand, but he chose to cover the error by diverting the topic. "A relationship was maintained because I had learned how to save space for grace."[clx] Perhaps what made the woman such an effective spokesperson is what she did NOT say when she talked to the men of the city about meeting Jesus. By leaving space for grace, she role modeled an entire cluster of proven leadership practices. Extending space for grace to others is the fundamental concept of an authentic leader. With our main character, the conclusion is this, "For her, this means that she can name her truth, she can receive truth about herself, and she is free to worship God without the burden of having to be in the "right place" and on the "right mountain." By claiming her authentic self, by receiving the gift of Living Water, there is no right or wrong place to worship. Wherever she is there is freedom."[clxi]

Let us look at one other group in our Bible story – the disciples. John 4:27-38 includes a conversation between the disciples and Jesus. Their focus never raised above a natural appetite. Despite walking with Jesus in ministry and standing as eyewitnesses to many miracles, they did not catch the cues of what was taking place between Jesus and the woman. They dismissed their thought process that is described as *marveling* and put their attention on whether Jesus needed to eat a meal. Using the exegetical analysis of narrative criticism, we find ourselves inside of the story and not mere observers. In the application of sovereign reign, your role as a leader is to ensure that your followers do not miss the cues of change. You are the change agent. You are the one that brings innovation to the table. Innovation is not about thinking; it is about constructing something new that gets the attention of others. Schrage (2000) considers innovation a level of playing. "Serious play is about improvising the unanticipated in ways that create new value."[clxii] Play is not a child-only realm. "Truly, I say to you, whoever does not receive the kingdom of God like a child shall not enter it" (Mark 10:15). Children learn by playing. Adults value play, but we tend to call it recreation to give it a more mature meaning. What did you play as a child that has translated into your career?

Brief Interjection

I was a tomboy as a child. I played with my brothers. I had a great hook shot, could climb higher in the tree, and was brave at the doctor's office. I had dolls, but I never played "mommy." I played teacher. I took my books and set them up on the floor to serve as desks and put my dolls and stuffed toys behind their desks. What is fascinating to me, in retrospect, is that there was no special education when I was a child. I mean nothing demeaning by the terms I am going to use; they simply reflect the terminology of that time. People were considered normal, crippled, or retarded. Of my dolls, one of them was crippled and one was retarded. When I would teach my class, I asked my retarded doll a question and then would admonish the class, "Give her time. She has an answer." When we had recess, I always told them to be patient with my crippled doll as she was to be included. Perhaps the presence of my grandmother's sister who had Down's Syndrome helped me develop that inclusiveness or the presence of my mother's sister who was visually impaired encouraged me to not think differently about people of varying levels of ability. One of my children spent some years in special education for the emotionally handicapped. After many moments of frustration, I sat down and laughed at myself realizing, "God, he is exactly who you made him to be, so he is 100 percent perfect. It is ME that needs help, Lord. I need to learn how to be his mother." Back to our conversation -

In retrospect, many of us read the story of John as if Jesus' request for a drink was His opening line to persuade her to the conversation about living water. If that is the case, then we assume that Jesus was operating in divinity rather than humanity.

Considering the author's writing style, remember that his gospel opens with a portrait of the Jesus as the Word *becoming* flesh. Jesus did not put on flesh like a costume to disguise His divinity. He *became* flesh. "Jesus experiences a full range of emotions, including grief (John 11:33-35), fatigue (John 4:6), anguish (John 12:27; 13:21), irritation (John 2:4; 6:26; 7:6-8; 8:25), irritation (John 2:3; 6-26; 7:6-8; 8:25), and suspicion (John 2:24-25). He remains thoroughly human as well as divine."[clxiii] How does this have value to the seventh dimension of leadership? John's gospel is reflective of a worldview consistent with the demands of 21st-century leadership. More than ever before, those in leadership must have a balance between their personal self and their leadership position. There can be dichotomy for purposes of contrast, but there cannot be a contradiction.

How do we arrive at sovereign reign? We get there by recognizing our diminishing self. Maggie Ross (1987) refers to it as *kenosis*. A kenotic experience is more than emptying of ourselves; it is, ". . . a self-emptying life that makes a person one with God, or rather allows God to enter in so that in a very real way one becomes and pours out the power of God."[clxiv] People who are facing death are no longer concerned with the accessories of life. The presence of death tends to strip off the trinkets and perks and put a clear perspective of only what is most important. For Jesus, one of those valued ambitions was that we would be one with the Father to the same degree that He was one with the Father. *Kenosis* is not an event; *kenosis* is dynamic. "It implies unending, self-emptying and out-pouring."[clxv] Our society is driven by what we can accumulate, so the willingness to engage in kenosis is in direct contradiction to secular ambitions. There must be not just an ambition but a revelation that kenosis does not result in a loss but a lively exchange. One statement from Ms. Ross' work completely changed my consideration of prayer.

> "People are sometimes so anxious to experience God in prayer that the mistake the technique they have been taught (or the body's response to that technique) for the encounter they seek."[clxvi]

In sovereign reign, we do not become subjects of a denominational definition of spirituality, but we become kingdom citizens. At the time that I read Ms. Ross' statement concerning prayer, I was a member of an Apostolic Pentecostal church where exuberance, speaking in tongues, and volume were some of the measuring tools for spiritual depth. It was quite a shift from my Catholic roots, and that is another story for another time. In the end, it was my addictive nature that was being fed which deprived me of the kenosis that was possible. God used the church to wound me deeply enough that I finally learned the lesson – God is God. Like many young believers of any denomination, I had inadvertently turned the church and my brothers and sisters in Christ into a form of idolatry. I became addicted to church. Thankfully, God wanted more for me and refused to let me miss out on the kinetic potential of sovereign reign. It is my testimony to encourage other leaders that God is not merely asking you to give away part of yourself. He asking you to trust Him enough to be willing to empty out. Here is the outcome of kenosis, "The self is no longer conscious of the need for boundaries because it has been found in the boundless God."[clxvii] That is the ultimate description of sovereign reign.

Application

Before we consider the application of sovereign reign, consider our dashboard.

Figure 8.1. Seventh Dimension Leadership Dashboard

Source: Williams, 2016

Remember that the dashboard is a means of monitoring systems. Is the temperature in the average range? Is the fuel level compatible to the distance intended for travel? Some of the monitoring is to note what is *not* showing any signs. The oil light blinking is a signal of concern. The seatbelt warning is a signal of reminder. For some functions, we must check the owner's manual or communicate with an expert. Consulting others is not a reflection of poor ownership, rather it reflects responsible stewardship.

In the Catholicism of my childhood, we were told that only Catholics are going to heaven. I used to think, "That is a LOT of people going to hell." It did not seem practical that God would create so many people and only allow a few into heaven. Part of my adulthood was within the Apostolic Pentecostal world where Acts 2:38 was the salvation standard and only those who complied were going to heaven. Once again, "That is a LOT of people going to hell." That conclusion was like a factory owner producing a massive quantity of parts and throwing most the parts away as scrap. The theology of determining a select group for heaven always seemed troublesome. Sovereign reign is not a lightweight commitment. It is not a Romans 10:9 confession that, "Jesus is Lord, so I am okay." The business world is filled with contractual agreements; however, sovereign reign is based on covenant promise. It is a marriage of the natural to the spiritual with a pledge of enduring commitment. The scenario at the well is classic to those in leadership. "[Ministers] are called to leave their own prejudices [at the cross] and to dispel any prejudices that will block the hearts of those they help . . . Our social location and ethnic identity should not dam or determine the flow of living water . . ."clxviii

Application of sovereign reign as an administration is a long-term commitment. If this section was a consultant's report, it would include recommendations for a series of seminars, partnering with Human Resources to begin the process at recruitment, setting initiatives with the Training Department for inclusion in annual training, and a communications strategy to saturate the organization with supportive messages to reinforce the value of sovereign reign. Does that mean that you print posters with scripture and disperse them throughout your organization? Clearly, that is not an option in our diverse society. This is not about proselytizing. It is about using the principles of biblical truths to make the world better. Moving beyond the woman at the well, let us consider the narrator of her story. The Gospel of St. John carries a unique theme of believing. Of the 143 times that the word *believe* is used by scriptural writers, 52 of them are contained in John's gospel. The story is not exclusively the woman's story as it is the inclusive story of a whole village who was persuaded to become believers. The woman had to be persuaded of her story before she could step into anyone else's story. Ching-Hsiang (2010) offers a five-part formula for leadership but clarifies that the only means to actively operate in the five begins, ". . . with inclusion of a positive force, a self-igniting spark that extends energy to the five factors that are interrelated, interlocked, and interdependent."[clxix] The five facets of leadership that are promoted include:

Figure 8.2. Five Elements of Leadership

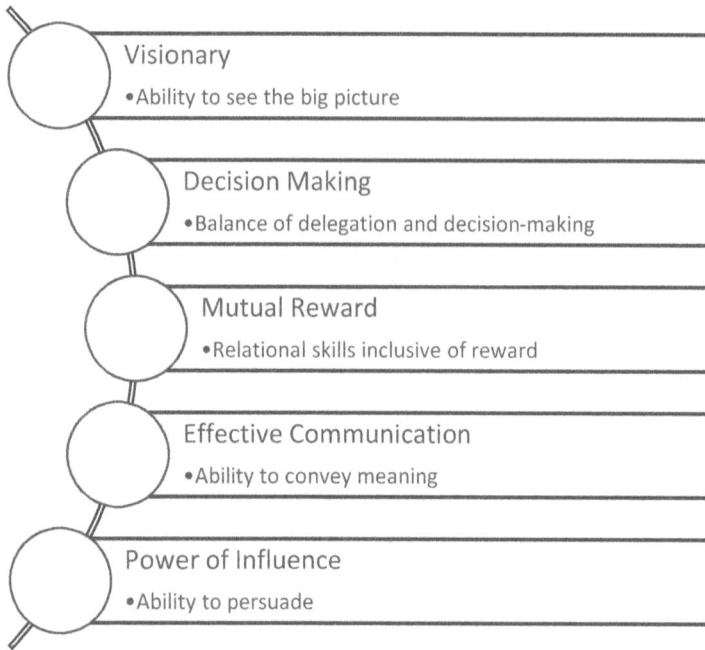

Visionary
- Ability to see the big picture

Decision Making
- Balance of delegation and decision-making

Mutual Reward
- Relational skills inclusive of reward

Effective Communication
- Ability to convey meaning

Power of Influence
- Ability to persuade

Source: Ching-Hsiang, 2010

One other contribution from Ching-Hsiang (2010) is the inclusion of three principles of leadership. These three collectively become the fundamental dynamic for leadership potential.

Figure 8.3. Three Principles of Leadership

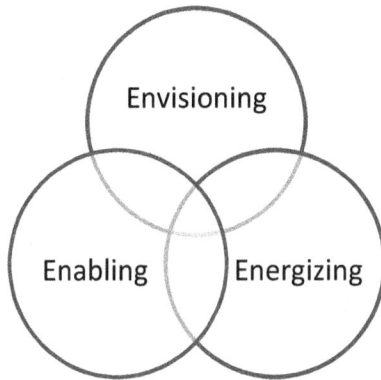

Source: Ching-Hsiang, 2010

Those three e's are inseparable. To take them apart is like driving a car on a flat tire. The whole vehicle becomes imbalanced. Visionary leaders generate vision in others. Visionary leaders are those who stir the people around them to move toward creative and constructive actions. Jesus provided the ultimate succession plan when He confirmed that a Comforter (John 14:26) would come for His followers and that they could be expected to be empowered (Acts 1:8). Vi

What is it about your life that should not be misinterpreted as only your story? What about your journey was designed to influence whole groups of people? Which point in your life became your shift from drawing natural water to becoming a consumer of living water? How did God prepare you for who you are now? When I think of my lifetime, God has always prepared me to be a strategic thinker. As a child, I loved to play strategy-based games with my siblings. I loved playing Stratego with my oldest brother. Even in games like baseball, I never just played in the outfield. I studied the batter and their body position and the way they held the bat to calculate where the ball was going to go if the batter hit it. When I drive, I play mathematical calculation games in my head such that I can typically estimate my arrival time within five minutes or less, even for trips of several hours. It is a worthwhile exercise to map your life, both chronologically and narratively, to discover the patterns of how you became the you of today. When we consider sovereign reign, it is a mapping of the woman at the well and the whole of humanity. It is a means of identifying the process of the journey until we arrive at the cathartic moment of allowing Jesus to become our identifier. It is only then that innocence, conscience, authority, promise, law, and grace can be placed within the context of sovereign reign.

Competency development is essential to having a functional succession plan. In the scriptures, Jesus trained His followers to continue the ministry. One of the first considerations of this book is that we must learn how to be leaders who are Christian. Biblical principles become our infrastructure. Rothwell (2010) recommends a two-part competency strategy. The first is a generic competency development strategy, such as offering a course or recommending articles on general practices. The second is a corporate-culture-specific development strategy. That takes place through a more exact connection such as, ". . . identify exemplary performers – individuals who are particularly good at demonstrating a competency."[clxx] Jesus modeled this strategy by having a general set of competencies that He imparted to the disciples, and then a specific strategy for the smaller group of Peter, James, and John. They were made privy to various miracles and teachings that were separate from the larger group.

Rothwell's work also offers a model for implementing learning objectives. Sovereign reign makes full use of every lesson that has accumulated in our journey. Consider the following three components for building effective objectives:

- *Resources. What equipment, tools, information, or other resources must be provided for the learner to demonstrate the necessary knowledge, skills, or abilities?*
- *Criteria. How will achievement of learning objectives be measured?*
- *Conditions. Under what conditions must the learner perform?*[clxxi]

In the sixth chapter of John's gospel, we find the narrative of the mass feeding. Before the miracle, Jesus asks Phillip what his ideas are on feeding such a crowd. Phillip did some quick math and told Jesus they could not afford to feed the group. "But this He said to **test** him, for He Himself knew what He would do" (John 6:6). During the years of working on a four-year degree, one of my instructors said, "A good teacher never stops teaching. From a good teacher, even the test teaches." It has become my experience to add a piece to that quote. "A masterful teacher knows how to learn from those they instruct." As a seventh-dimension leader, remain proactive in developing activities and instruction for your team. Be sure that you are learning from those you teach. As you move into the place where you are the one preparing someone to succeed you, set lofty goals for how the person following you will exceed your achievements. "Most assuredly, I say to you, he who believes in Me, the works that I do he will do also; and greater works than these he will do, because I go to My Father" (John 14:12). "If your organization uses the same recruitment strategies as most other organizations, then you will get about the same results as those other organizations do."[clxxii]

Reading Between the Lines

What could possibly be said about reading between the lines after the seventh dimension? Please allow me to start with a confession. After completing this document and receiving confirmation from Regent University that I do indeed have a doctorate, my 2009 Buick Enclave started making funny noises. My washing machine broke. I received a letter from the IRS about my non-profit New Day Ministries. I had to clean out my file cabinet to locate transcripts to include with a resume. In the file cabinet, I found a folder of information from a ministry called Sozo (Greek for healing). Inside the folder were two pieces of legal pad paper folded and stuck in a pocket. They contained questions and observations from the ministers who had a session with me.

There were reminders to put my armor on before anything and to dust off anything that was ungodly and to take God seriously.

There was a note to not only close the door of fear but to put caulking around it. Bingo! I am not much on building things. Nevertheless, I have noted that caulking can become dried and cracked and periodically needs replaced. Those events I told you about had released a simmering fear from years ago, that a domino effect was beginning to undo all the good that has happened. For any step forward, two steps backward were inevitable. I am facing monumental student loans, and I felt the fear of being old and poor and on and on and on. My drama queen personality was tapping my spiritual doorway to find the old caulking and break the seal.

In the seventh dimension of leadership, we must be fully committed to not re-engaging old mindsets and old behaviors. The Apostle Paul understood that when he wrote, "Therefore if any man be in Christ, he is a new creature: old things are passed away; behold, all things are become new" (2 Corinthians 5:17). It is as simple as unplugging a cord from a socket. We love the concept of empowerment, but there are some things in life that we need to dis-empower. Pull the plug on every mindset that is not compatible to your destiny!

Seventh-dimensional leaders are calm(er) and understand that decisions are the result of timing and planning. My mother used to tell me, "Your first children get your energy. Your last children get your wisdom." I confess that I spanked my older children. Someone offered a book on parenting to me, and I recognized that my motivation for spanking was not correction but as an outlet because I was angry at their behavior. It took a LOT of prayer and commitment to alter my parenting style concerning correction. With my youngest daughter, I was likely to say, "I am too upset with you to make good decisions right now. Go to your room, and we will address this later."

I also learned to remove myself from the situation and walk away when needed. Instead of giving orders, we held weekly family business meetings where my children made choices about how they would contribute to the household in the upcoming week. By empowering them, I calmed our environment. If the one that chose to clean the bathroom started grumbling in the middle of the week, they had no reason to be upset with me. I would say, "You chose the task, and you may renegotiate at the next meeting." I also mastered a problem-solving model called "your problem, my problem, no problem."

For example, if one of my children came into the living room and said they could not find any socks, that is only my problem if they do not own any socks. I used an effective response of, "Since I bought and launder your socks, finding the socks is your problem. You are very intelligent, and I am sure you will be fine locating them." A child that came to me in another part of our apartment to ask, "Mom, do we have any ketchup" gained this response, "You are very intelligent, and I am sure you are well able to move a few things around and locate ketchup." My problem, your problem, no problem? Seventh-dimensional leaders know that this is forever a growing process. There is no "happily ever after" ending, because there is no ending. Lineage and posterity are activated in this dimension. It is not about our name, title, or reputation. It is about what we impart to others that will continue to increase in generations. Be memorable!

Chapter 9

Summary

What are the takeaways from this book? My first hope is that readers find spiritual and intellectual stimulation. Prayerfully, the content has sparked thought processes about the stages of your life and how to bring those to the leadership experience. Whether your journey has been primarily on the smoothness and speed of an interstate or the bumps and jerks of a gravel road, periodically we will find ourselves at common intersections. While many of my friends have been lovely people all their lives that is not my story. I quit high school because of a rebellious and rowdy lifestyle of drugs, alcohol, sexual promiscuity, crime, and so on (fill in the blank). After having four children by three different men and becoming embedded into a cycle of poverty, I went to night school and finished high school. Following many more challenges in life, I started college classes. The first time an instructor pointed to me and asked, "What do you think" I froze. What do I think? Think? Because of a relationship with such domestic violence and abuse to the degree that, at one point in my life, I did not laugh without permission, I had surrendered the ability to think. Suddenly, this person was asking me to do what I thought had been taken away from me forever. Taking a deep breath and shaking off my terror, I answered the question. With some humor, I can say I am still telling people what I think to this day!

It took 18 years to finish a 4-year degree. The darkness of life nearly swallowed me whole, but there was just enough light that I never completely gave up. Battling anxiety attacks and depression and many other struggles repeatedly pushed me to the brink. By the time I graduated with a Bachelor's in General Studies from Indiana University East, I had grandchildren yelling from the audience as I walked across the stage, "Yeah, Nanny!" Soon after, the education bug bit me again, and I enrolled at Indiana Wesleyan University for a master's degree in Strategic Management. I set a personal goal and completed that degree in 18 months with straight A's. I wanted to grab as much as I could from every single book and every professor. More than what I wanted from the experience; I had a passion for giving to others. I wanted others, like you, to have hope and inspiration and an adventurous spirit to embrace knowledge and enjoy challenges. When I think of teaching, I frame it is an opportunity to inspire others for having a passion to learn. As adjunct faculty for two business colleges, I often have adult students who have the intelligence but are not sure that they deserve to be a student. I completely understand that mindset, so I view my teaching mission to be as much about motivation and encouragement as it is about the course materials.

One thing life has taught me well is that this is not a contest. We are not competing with one another. I should be able to cheer you on when you are operating in excellence. To be threatened or intimidated by someone else's achievement is a very loud statement of insecurity. I had a supervisor many years ago that came to work upset because the suit she had bought for a speaking engagement was wrinkled. Her purchase came from a high-end department store. She was upset that she had not looked inside the suit bag until it was too late to send the suit out for pressing. Suddenly, she stopped and said, "Oh, Kathy, I am ashamed. When I think about how you struggle day-to-day, what right do I have to complain about a suit?" What? I immediately responded, "For you, a wrinkled suit is a legitimate challenge. You have no need to apologize for the challenges in your world, even if they are different than what challenges me." Please allow me to throw in a Williams' interpretation of the commandment that we are not supposed to covet. It is too easy to think that scripture means that I want what you have or vice versa. Coveting goes much deeper than that. Coveting is wanting to take possession of what someone else owns to the extent that it is as if they never had it all, and it was always in your possession. Coveting is a deep psychological (and sinful) mindset of taking over parts of someone else's life.

What else do I hope you take from this book? I hope that you take a zeal for creative thinking and innovation. My hope for you is that you reconsider the structure of leadership and have a willingness to give. I hope that you can close your own knowing-doing gap and, in turn, impart experience to your organization. Growing up in a big family meant that sharing was an expectation, for the good and bad. We shared clothes and toys and books. We also shared germs. When someone had the flu or a cold, it was expected that it was going to travel throughout the brothers and sisters. There were too many to think that what one had would not travel to others. Maybe I bring that big family mentality to everything I do, including sharing my journey and now, my learning. I want you to grab your fork and taste what is on my plate! Despite my picturesque narratives, learning is a serious passion that has my full dedication. A significant quality of effective leadership is taking responsibility for decision making. I noted a poster once that said, "Nothing messes up an apology worse than an excuse." As leaders, let us take excuse making off the table and own our flaws.

Once I tell this next story, you might not be so willing to share a meal with me, but please hear the moral of the story. Most of the years while I raised my children we lived in poverty, complete with food stamps that were issued in booklets. Overall, I managed our budget reasonably well by preparing home-cooked meals. On the last day of the month, we were down to a minimal amount of food. I decided to prepare salmon patties, fried potatoes, and corn. To set the scene, it is important to note that I have one daughter who is simply l-o-u-d. She is a screamer when she is angry or upset, and the story centers on her response to a situation. As we sat at the table to eat, she raised a forkful of fried potatoes to her mouth. In my peripheral vision, I noted that a cockroach had fried in with the potatoes. What to do? If I tell her about the invasion to her food, she was going to scream. That would end the meal for everyone, and there was nothing else to prepare. If I did not tell her, what kind of mother was I? As you can imagine, I had only a split second to decide. What to do? What would you do? Leadership includes making hard decisions that might negatively impact others – sometimes with little time to be thoughtful and consider all factors.

Through my work with a community center in Indianapolis, I had the opportunity to be certified as a conflict resolution and neighborhood mediation trainer. We worked with members of opposing gangs in efforts to bring peace to neighborhoods, particularly in summer months. With every workshop, I would do extensive preparation. Finally, one of the other trainers said, "At some point, you have to have confidence in what you know." If there is one compliment you can take away from this book, it is the encouragement to have confidence in what you know. Pause! What happened in the fried potato story? If you must know, I admit that I was on the verge of making the decision to let her eat it. Just as she was ready to put the bite in her mouth, she looked up and saw her brother watching me watching her. It was a visual pinball effect! In that ping-ping-ping moment, she saw it, threw her fork down, jumped up and screamed, "THERE IS A BUG IN MY FOOD!" At that point, I was laughing so hard that tears were rolling down my face. She stood and pointed at me yelling, "And YOU! You were going to let me eat it!" All I could do was nod my head affirmatively and claim the decision. If memory serves me correctly, we ate peanut butter sandwiches that night.

A primary pivot point in my life came when I let go of a question that had become internalized from childhood. "What is wrong with me?" is a question that causes a slow but sure psychological and spiritual death. For me, it started taking root in childhood, although I grew up in a very normal family. At the time of my mother's death in 2015, my parents were within weeks of their 67th wedding anniversary. There is nothing about my story that is based on pointing fingers at them or anyone else. The struggle that was taking place in my own head was fed by external situations until I did not know how to be me. When God began to deliver me from anxiety attacks, one of the issues He pinpointed for me is that I did not know how to trust me with me. Over a period of time, I developed some practices that alleviated and finally eliminated the panic attacks. A friend asked me once, "When you look in the mirror, who do you see?" I encourage you to take that question and personalize it. Go to the mirror and ask yourself that question. Stand there and look deeply into the "you" that is looking back from the mirror. Work your way up to saying out loud what you like about you. Are there reflections of innocence, conscience, authority, promise, law, or grace that are trying to crowd into the mirror with you? Be patient. They will dissipate and finally, you will be able to answer, "I see me."

Seventh dimension leadership is not about perfection but about maturity and thoroughness. It includes past-present-future elements. Dr. Gary Oster's advocacy for elegance is a seventh dimension leadership quality. "Elegant solutions seem deceptively simple, yet they solve immensely complex problems once and for all time without introducing any new problems. Elegant solutions are based on universal laws that will not be affected by changes in circumstances related to time and place. If it is elegant, it will always and everywhere be true."[clxxiii] The first six dimensions are the opportunity to learn how to travel. By the seventh dimension, the more seasoned traveler understands that one pair of pants and three different tops are the makings of three outfits. With the use of the hotel laundry, baggage is reduced to a carry-on item. It is about packing efficiently rather than extensively. Efficiency is supported by credibility, and credibility is the quality that will inspire others to elegant solutions. Per Hackman and Johnson (2013), there are six elements of building credibility. They are:

Figure 9.0. Elements of Building Credibility

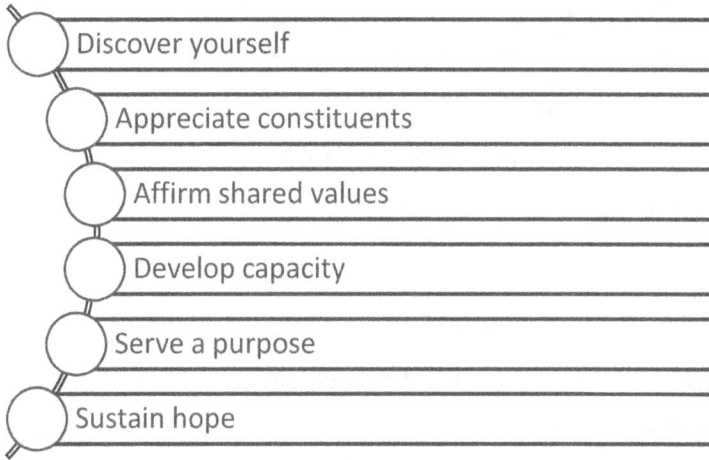

- Discover yourself
- Appreciate constituents
- Affirm shared values
- Develop capacity
- Serve a purpose
- Sustain hope

Source: Hackman & Johnson, 2013

These six elements closely parallel our six dimensions that culminate in a seventh dimension of credibility. A person who has mastered credibility is a person who has mastered self-discovery. "The jack-of-all-trades is a bungler in every one of them."[clxxiv] Reaching the seventh dimension is a tribute to discovering destiny. It is your calling. It is the reason you have a story. It is the climactic moment in the script of life. It is the destination of your earthly journey.

Samuel Regenstrief (Sammy to his friends and workers) moved to the United States to escape the emerging Nazi movement in the 1930's. Through a series of events, he became the owner of Design & Manufacturing, Corp. (D&M) in Connersville, IN.[clxxv] For many years, D&M dominated the manufacturing of dishwashers. The company ultimately closed following his retirement. Do we remember Regenstrief for making dishwashers in a small Midwestern city? Most have no idea of his name, yet millions have been direct recipients of his genius. The Austrian immigrant took the methodical looping technique of the manufacturing world and applied it to medical record keeping in a way the revolutionized the field. The Regenstrief Medical Record System (RMRS), implemented in 1972, has breathtaking impact, including, "Over 10.5 million distinct patients, 2 billion clinical results/observations, 36 million full-text reports (including diagnostic studies, procedure results, operative notes, and discharge summaries), and 140 million radiology images have been entered into the system."[clxxvi] Where is your curiosity taking you? What adventure awaits you tinkering with one idea and wondering how to apply it to a unique problem? Whose life (or how many lives) will be impacted by you making the connection between dishwashers and medical records?

In the seventh dimension, a woman who had no social worth became the voice that carried a life-changing message to a city. The longer I live, the more I accept that life rarely works out per a specific blueprint. There seem to be a chosen few who have mapped their journey and can walk through that plan with minimal disruption. Many of us can relate to Peter who spent his life as a fisherman and suddenly felt compelled to leave it all and follow Jesus. There are those pivots in life when we just know that we know that we are supposed to take a new route. Some of us can relate to Paul's shift from Saul and his all-out commitment to a cause until a moment of revelation turns his energy to what appears to be a contradictory purpose. He went from persecuting believers to becoming one of the great leaders in the New Testament. The Bible is full of stories that are valuable to those of us living in this 21st-century world of rapid turns and twists. While we live in a world brimming with opportunities, we also live in a world that appears to be spinning out of control. Is global warming waiting on you to pivot? Has the cure for cancer or HIV been just out of reach until you make the needed connections? Is there an organization that needs you to be their woman at the well and inspire whole groups to change their mentality?

One of the primary advantages to arriving at the seventh dimension is that it is a place where all the pieces of the puzzle become meaningful. It is the collective good that provides that meaning. It did not "feel" good to have many of the situations that took place in my life, but it became my responsibility to find the good in every circumstance. As an example, I can either focus on the prejudice and racism that my children and I experienced from within the church, or I can benefit from the spiritual disciplines that resulted. My commitment to prayer, fasting and studying the Word came from years of feeling that God was the only one I could cry out to for help or understanding. Today, I celebrate pain, because it became the catalyst for spiritual depth. The blame game is meaningless. I can fault myself for my early recklessness and then look at my family background and then my ancestry and work my way all the back to Eden, and to what end? It is more beneficial to put that energy into doing well in the present and preparing for the future. In the seventh dimension, you have gathered your experiences and invested them toward becoming a master thinker. Master thinkers are reflective thinkers.

Figure 9.1. Stages of Critical Thinking

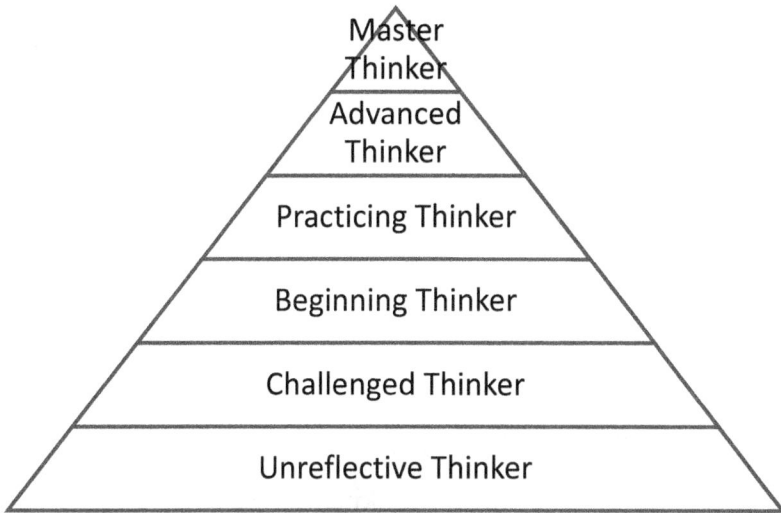

Source: Paul & Elder, 2006

When I was a freshman in high school, my Spanish teacher told everyone on the first day of class that he would not award an A+ no matter what the quality of work. He said that because Spanish was not our native language, that it was not possible for us to deserve an A+. He said that no matter how well we did, we still had to process the language of Spanish through an English-speaking mind. An A+ said that I not only understood Spanish and could speak Spanish, but that I think in Spanish. That is a lesson that I took into my Christian walk as early in my walk, my choice to do good was first processed through my carnal mind. For instance, my choice not to cuss was first processed through a cussing mindset (one small example). A master thinker has learned to that their actions are the result of skillful and insightful thinking. All of us started at the bottom of the pyramid. With unreflective thinking, "We walk about the world with confidence that things really are the way they appear to us."[clxxvii] Challenged thinking is the embryonic stage of reflective thinking, e.g. reconsidering cigarette smoking. The beginning thinker is in a stage of recognizing their egocentric patterns. "A thinker who has never challenged his own thinking has no right to challenge the thinking of others."[clxxviii] Master thinking thrives on systems thinking with a balance of analytic and creative approaches. One path to arriving at master thinking is to have a relationship with your mind. We cannot stumble into this relationship more than we could with another human being. It is easy to shrug the mind into the category of unconscious relationship, but that leaves too much to happenstance. "The best thinkers make that unconscious relationship conscious and deliberate."[clxxix]

"Successful leaders are learners. And the learning process is ongoing, a result of self-discipline and perseverance."[clxxx] While it is idealistic, I have often said that a person who reads is capable of learning anything. In my prayers, it is my custom to thank God not only for being literate but to read with comprehension. "Today, nearly 17% of the world's adult population is still not literate; two-thirds of them women, making gender equality even harder to achieve."[clxxxi] I completely credit my upbringing and the disciplines of a parochial education for laying a solid foundation in my life. Despite my wrecking-ball years of hedonism, there was a foundation laid that allowed for reconstruction. The harsh reality is that, as a young person, some of my drug use could have resulted in my mind breaking. The undeserved mercies of God allowed me to transition back to a lifestyle of purpose. The title of a keynote speech that I delivered at a graduation was, "The 'F' word." I spoke of how my command of English had deteriorated into a swampland of cursing, particularly the "F" word. I used it as the subject and verb. It was a word that caused fights and made peace. It was the alpha and omega of my younger self. I still use the "F" word, only now it stands for future.

Effective leaders have a passion for looking ahead, ". . . take stock of their present positions and anticipate what lies beyond the horizon – to scan their environment."[clxxxii] It is reasonable to suggest that the entire Christian experience is constructed as an exercise in futuring. Why else would God have positioned The Revelation in the 66th position? Futuring is a historian's dream. "Futurists, like historians, must examine events in a large and complex context."[clxxxiii] Millett (2011) presents five practices of futuring, including consideration of complementary views and analytics. There is too much at stake for leaders to not be equipped for not only moving ahead but looking ahead. Inclusion of a Training and Development (T&D) component to your Human Resource Department is not excessive. Even a 5-year projection is highly limited in scope for the contemporary world of business. Every person on an executive team should possess the skills set for future planning. At minimum that includes:

- *Projecting trends;*
- *Visualizing possible and probable futures; and*
- *Drawing implications.*[clxxxiv]

While I did not include an "Application" section in this chapter, it is a worthwhile suggestion to pose that futuring takes practice and is a worthwhile investment for the organization to invest in consultancy and training.

Operating in the seventh dimension of leadership speaks volumes about your character. It says that you are not only bold and strong, but you are sensitive and caring. You have closed the gap between intended behavior and actual behavior. Seventh dimension leadership testifies that you are comfortable with your mistakes, and even more, your failures. These were our high dives that let us leap into the deep end of the swimming pool. We have a responsibility to be in awe of God. I was raised in a small Midwestern town where 13th Street was the highest numbered street. When jets appeared in the sky, they were only small white dots in the far distance. Occasionally, one was low enough to see its shape, and in a rare instance, I could make out the TWA on the plane's tail. As a child, I often wondered if the people inside of those planes were appreciative of their privilege of being in the air when that is a place God reserved for birds. To this day, I will stop and watch when a plane flies overhead. Any night that I walk outside, I look up to see where the moon is in the sky. Keep yourself elevated above what is taking place in your immediate surroundings. Have a point of "looking up" that provides inner peace. When life becomes jumbled, I go one of two places. I take long drives in the country to watch nature. A cornfield must do only one thing to be successful – grow corn. To make that happen, it needs only three things – soil, water, and the sun. God reminds me that life is not as complex as we believe it is. The second place that I go is the airport. I watch the planes take off, and I am reminded that I am not only watching the impossible happen, it is happening with power. "Jesus said to him, "If you can believe, all things *are* possible to him who believes" (Mark 9:23). Each of us needs a set of reminders that God is with us. "Behold, the virgin shall be with child, and bear a Son, and they shall call His name Immanuel," which is translated, "God with us" (Matthew 1:23). Develop some personal mechanisms that un-jumble your world. Use them like an over-the-counter pill, "take as needed."

There is an expression about having the best of both worlds, but when it comes to seventh dimension leadership, you get the best of all dispensations. You are gifted at moving others to see possibility. You are qualified to challenge beliefs and assumptions and package the challenges with inspiration. ". . . strategic thinking involves a collective dimension as well as an individual one."[clxxxv] The collective dimension of the dispensations looks like this:

Figure 9.2. Collective Dimension of Seven Dispensations

DISPENSATION	CHARACTERISTIC	DISPENSATIONIONAL CHALLENGE	SEVENTH DIMENSION FEATURE
Innocence	No preconceived ideas, absence of history	Naive, vulnerability, false security	Experiential, change and innovation
Conscience	Distinguishes right from wrong	Personal interpretation	Critical thinking, self-awareness
Authority	Control from disorder, unification in planning	Groupthink	Leadership style, collaborative influence
Promise	Hope	Interpersonal dependency	Interpersonal, long-term planning
Law	Firmness, Solidification	Superseding of Spirit, Inflexibility	Accountability and liability, setting parameters
Grace	Capacity	Privilege without commitment	Empathy, relational skills
Sovereign Reign	Wholeness, clarity, visionary, strategic, diversity, agility, comprehensive, inclusive, communicative	Lifelong learner to continue growth and advancement	Cumulative of first six dimensions plus a holistic vitality

Source: Williams, 2016

Another way of visualizing this is to consider it as an orchestration with Sovereign Reign as the conductor. Each one of the instruments in an orchestra has individual expertise, but it is the blending of their sounds that raises the bar to a brilliance that cannot be achieved in a solo. In the seventh dimension, the instruments of each of your dispensations are gathered together and capable of producing a symphony of sound. Seventh dimension leadership is equivalent to the arts. Whether you are musical, artistic, or a writer, find the venue that allows you to flourish in leadership expression. David says in Psalm 45:1, "My heart is inditing a good matter: I speak of the things which I have made touching the king: my tongue *is* the pen of a ready writer." Visions are only dreams without the impartation of communication. The seventh dimension of leadership is a mastery of self and having self in correct priorities. Seventh-dimensional leaders have their spiritual beliefs as their center. The spirit guides the soul which is reflected in the physical realm. No wonder that Paul confessed, "for 'In him we live and move and have our being'; as even some of your poets have said, 'For we are indeed his offspring' (Acts 17:28, NKJV). The key to seventh dimension leadership is an upward version of the credit effective leaders gives to their teams. "But we have this treasure in earthen vessels, that the excellence of the power may be of God and not of us" (2 Corinthians 4:7).

Brief Interjection

Sometimes we struggle, not because of the actual wound, but because of scar tissue. Medically, scar tissue is the result of the body rushing collagen to the point of injury. Let's consider it from a spiritual perspective. In our previous injuries of the first six dispensations, we have coping mechanisms thus emotional, spiritual, and psychological collagen rushes to the scene. They are necessary critical interventions that close the wound. Yet, God is saying to us, "You have only trusted me for the initial phase of the process. You left me out of the rehabilitation. You have completely negated the necessity of rehabilitation. Little wonder then that just like the prophet Jeremiah's words, even though there is healing and balm, the health of the daughter of my people is not recovered" (Jeremiah 8:22).

If we go to Peter, despite being on the Mount of Transfiguration and witnessing revelation, he could not HANDLE revelation. Peter's response to the vision of animals being lowered to him was in Acts 10:14, "Not so, Lord." In a question that many might view as heresy, over 20 years ago, I asked this question,

"What if being Spirit-filled isn't enough?" Acts 4:8 specifically describes Peter as *"filled with the Holy Ghost."* It was not until Acts 10:28 when Peter learned to confess, *"God showed me"* that the scar tissue was finally worked away from the wound of inadequacy and back out into the skin tissue. His movement became unrestricted by what had happened in the past. What used to be a wound has become a part of the testimony. What used to be the display of an old wound became a signature of wholeness. It is only when we have wholeness that we can ascend.

Perhaps an even more relevant model is Jesus. *"Jesus saith unto her, Touch me not; for I am not yet ascended to my Father: but go to my brethren, and say unto them, I ascend unto my Father, and your Father; and to my God, and your God"* (John 20:17). Perhaps we can consider that Jesus needed the additional time on earth to ensure that there would be no scar tissue limitations to His mission. Earlier in His ministry, Jesus said he wanted us to be like Jesus and the Father and be one? What was for him is for us? Ascension is for us. What does ascension mean? It means that I can freely go to the Father. It means that I am not restricted by this realm of existence. It means I can go beyond what has been in the past and function in wholeness. Paul said in Romans 10:6 (KJV), *"But the righteousness which is of faith speaketh on this*

wise, Say not in thine heart, Who shall ascend into heaven? (that
is, to bring Christ down from above:) Ascension is bringing Christ
down to where we exist. When we get Christ into where we live,
we have completed the wholeness process. We are no longer in
need of coping mechanisms because we operate out of
competencies.

Seventh-dimension leaders have developed resonance.
Newberg's work on world-class performers is summarized under
the label of an *experiential* dream. "They are willing to work very
hard for what they want; they feel a strong sense of personal
responsibility for creating the freedoms they wish to enjoy; they all
encountered major obstacles . . .."[clxxxvi] Mature resonance is not
about a feel-good experience as illicit sex and illegal drugs would
then fall into that category. There is no regretful morning after
with legitimate resonance. Clawson (2009) uses this four-step
model of resonance as a framework:

Figure 9.3. The Purpose of Life

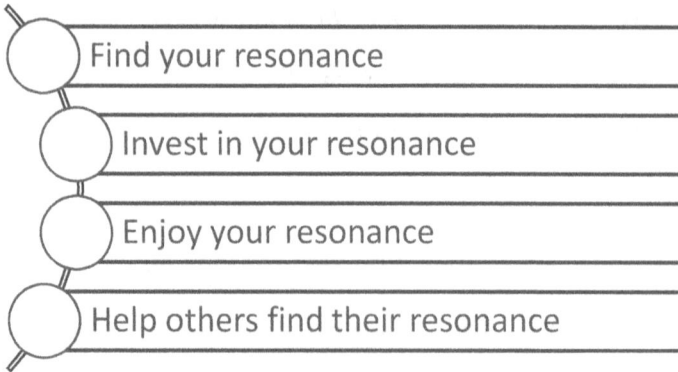

◯	Find your resonance
◯	Invest in your resonance
◯	Enjoy your resonance
◯	Help others find their resonance

Source: Clawson, 2009

"The notion of resonance and resonant leadership is based on a principle of physics that describes the generation of sound of musical instruments. Instruments all have natural frequencies at which they are capable of vibrating if they are struck, strummed, or blown at the appropriate frequency. When one object vibrating at the same natural frequency of a second sets the second into vibrational motion, you have resonance. And you get music."[clxxxvii]

Resonance is the reason we hear sounds in a seashell. Leaders need emotional resonance with their team. It is the reason people are elected to public office as there is a similarity of "sound" in the discussion of various issues. We see resonance demonstrated with laughter. Dissonance is the opposite and builds on negatives. There are moments when change is needed that resolute dissonance is helpful. Dissolute dissonance is never an asset to an organization or any grouping of people within a company. Those of us in leadership must have a mission to incorporate resonance in our surroundings.

In the seventh dimension of leadership, you are now on the mission field to identify recipients of your journey. It has become your quest to mentor others and applaud their growth. Use the miracle of loaves and fishes as your model. "Then he ordered the crowds to sit down on the grass, and taking the five loaves and the two fish he looked up to heaven, and blessed, and broke and gave the loaves to the disciples, and the disciples gave them to the crowds" (Matthew 14:19, RSV). Let go of the concerns for the resources that are not obvious, look to heaven, bless what you have, and start sharing. Let God be the multiplier of what you do have, and there is a guarantee of more than enough. You have a mastery that is deeply needed in the world of the 21st century. You have learned not just to become a Christian leader but a leader who is a Christian. "The grace of the Lord Jesus be with all the saints. Amen" (Revelation 22:21).

Reading Between the Lines

This is the closing story. A few years ago, I took a trip with my grandsons. Of course, the trip started with a fight about who would be in the front seat. The grandson that won the battle sat smugly with me wearing his "cool" shades and declaring to the others that he was the co-captain. If anyone needed to talk to the captain (me), they would need to go through him first. After a couple of hours of driving, he lowered his sunglasses on the tip of his nose, put his elbow on the armrest, and said, "So, Nanny, do all of your kids have the same dad?" I tried to divert him and said, "Your uncles have the same father" and proceeded to give him a little information, such as his service in the Vietnam War in the 101st Airborne. He didn't take the bait and proceeded to question me, "So, my Mom and Aunt Centa have the same dad?" Who put this prosecuting attorney in my van? I decided to give in and tell him. I spoke slowly and calmly, "No, your Mom and Aunt Centa do not have the same dad." He turned away from me briefly and then looked back (still looking over the top of his glasses) to say, "Dag, Nanny, that's three boyfriends. You was a play-uh!"

May I suggest that in our role of leadership, we not only have to have questioning mastered, but we have a responsibility to be questioned. Our life is an open book and transparency is our responsibility, even when it is uncomfortable. Does that mean we have no privacy? No, that is not the message. Offering clarity to those who team with us is essential. In The Message version of 2 Corinthians 3, Paul explains that we are the story, "Your very lives are a letter that anyone can read by just looking at you. Christ himself wrote it—not with ink, but with God's living Spirit; not chiseled into stone, but carved into human lives." Have a life that people can read and be better for what we have shared.

Postscript

I have said many times in life that if I could be anything I wanted to be, I would ask God to allow me to be an African griot. A griot explains the unexplainable by telling stories about it. The story of Anansi the spider is likely one of the best-known tales. Anansi is a story from Ghana about a spider who consistently got into trouble and used his wits and humor to get out of trouble. Now that I think about it, I am not sure if I would make a better griot or the Anansi? Anyway, I added this brief section as a bit of a personal disclaimer. As I worked toward completing this book, I realized that the stories that I have shared make me seem that I have it together. Believe me, that is nowhere near the truth! I could have easily shared an entire series of bungling poor decisions that caused consequences to unfold for years. While I am calm and patient now, in years past my temperament was attached to a short fuse and a critical mind. I judged people before they could judge me. Even in the growing process, I moved my criticisms from my words to my thoughts. It takes hard work to change.

Do you recall my story about using the "f" word? There was a time in my life that I nearly qualified for ESL (English as a Second Language) courses because cussing had become my native tongue. It took a dedicated effort to break away from the rapid-fire street language and make myself behave civilly. One of my techniques was to read billboards while I drove. "Burger King – you can have it your way." I enunciated again and again. Revelation 3:15-16, the issue with the Laodicean church is that they were not hot or cold in their works. What I have always read into that scripture is that God wants us to be decisive. Make a clear commitment and then stand on that as your truth. Mark 10:21 documents the conversation between Jesus and the rich young ruler. Jesus tells the young man to take up his cross and follow. I doubt that he literally meant a cross in the sense of a crucifixion, but the underlying message is to adopt a position and then live it. We cannot help anyone if we talk a good talk and have nothing to back up our words. Proverbs 25:14 says that people who boast and do not back it up are like clouds and wind with no rain. The determination you hear from me in this book did not come quickly and absolutely did not come easily. I freely confess that when I was young, I talked a lot but had little action to support my words.

While driving one of my mentors to run errands, I asked her, "If you had one piece of advice that you could give to this generation, what would it be? What is missing?" She immediately said, "Obedience. Folks nowadays don't know how to just obey.

Everyone wants to ask questions instead of just obeying." I do not believe she was referring to a blind compliance or removing dialogue. What she was saying is that we do not tap into the experience of others. With the trends toward leadership coaching, executive coaching, innovation, creative thinking, organizational culture, succession plans, mentoring, and much more, we have opportunity to be enriched by our workplace. Psalm 145:4 says, "One generation shall praise Your works to another, And shall declare Your mighty acts." The Bible contains almost 300 references to generation, generations, and heritage. If we look at the King James Version, we find the word *begat* 225 times.

Leadership is not a solo act. We are not a one-act play. This is an ongoing script that adds characters by generations. This is a collective experience. We live in an exciting time. Despite the sometimes-heavy responsibilities of leadership, it is the calling to make a difference that matters most of all. Herta Von Stiegel authored a book titled *The Mountain Within* (2011). Her book tells the story of her climb to the top of Mount Kilimanjaro and is filled with leadership lessons. She says, "Investing in your legacy is a powerful and potent action. When you look back and examine your life, you will want see that you did more than just grind your way to the top . . . After all, when you're gone, isn't it important that you will have contributed something to the world as a whole?"[clxxxviii]

Here is a prayer for you, the reader.

Dear Jesus, I am grateful for the opportunity that you have permitted to spend time in writing and sharing thoughts that I believe will encourage and uplift others. For every reader of this book, I pray that you will bless them with encouragement and inspiration. I pray that they have time to reflect and hear your voice as you guide them in leadership. Let their own story come alive and become effective in guiding others. For those experienced leaders who are reading, I pray for a fresh increase to their vision and mission. Help us collectively to hear your word and do your will. In the example that you set, Jesus, we pray that all the good we might do will glorify the Father. We willingly sit at your feet and say, "Teach us." Thank you for every blessing and each opportunity that you have extended to us. Thank you for the mercies that cover our mistakes and hope that allows us to improve. In your name, Amen.

References

Adams, N.E. (2015). Bloom's taxonomy of cognitive learning objectives. *Journal of The Medical Library Association*, 103(3), 152-153. doi:10.3163/1536-5050.103.3.010

Auer, M.R. (2011). The policy sciences of social media. *Policy Studies Journal*, 39(4), 709-736. doi:10.1111/j.1541-0072.2011.00428.x

Barrett, M. (2014). Are you a Control Freak? *Leadership Excellence Essentials*, 31(3), 28-29. Retrieved [Accessed on November 13, 2016] from EBSCOHost Database

Beckwith, C. A. (1911). The types of authority in Christian belief. *Harvard Theological Review*, 4(2), 241-252. Retrieved [Accessed on November 9, 2016] from EBSCOHost Database.

Bingham, N. W. (2012, April 11). Charles Spurgeon on Calvanism – irresistible grace. Retrieved from Ligonier Ministries Website at http://www.ligonier.org/blog/charles-spurgeon-calvinism-irresistible-grace/

Blanding, M. (2015, January 26). Workplace stress responsible for up to $190 billion in annual U.S. healthcare costs. Retrieved from *Forbes* Website at http://www.forbes.com/sites/hbsworkingknowledge/2015/0

1/26/workplace-stress-responsible-for-up-to-190-billion-in-annual-u-s-heathcare-costs/#19bbce2d4333

Business Utopia. (2016). retrieved from https://www.businesstopia.net/communication/psychologic al-barriers on October 5, 2016.

Breathnach, S. B. (2005). Simple Abundance. New York, NY: Grand Central Publishing.

Brown, S. (2015). Water imagery and the power and presence of God in the Gospel of John. *Theology Today* (Online), 72(3), 289-298. doi:10.1177/0040573615601471

Brown, S. (2015). What Is truth? Jesus, Pilate, and the staging of the dialogue of the cross in John 18:28-19:16a. *The Catholic Biblical Quarterly*, 77(1), 69-86. Retrieved [Accessed on November 13, 2016] from EBSCOHost Database.

Burgonito-Watson, T.B. (2005). Sexism and racial ethnic women in the church: a reflection on the Samaritan woman. *Church & Society*, 95(4), 89-93. Retrieved [Accessed on October 17, 2016] from EBSCOHost Database.

Cabrera, A. & Unruh, G. (2012). *Being Global: How to Think, Act, and Lead in a Transformed World*. Boston, MA: Harvard Business Review Press.

Caligiuri, P. (2012). *Cultural Agility: Building a Pipeline of Successful Global Professionals.* San Francisco, CA: Jossey-Bass.

Callahan, C. (2009). Resonance, dissonance, and leadership. *U.S. Army Medical Department Journal*, 32-36. Retrieved [Accessed on November 15, 2016] from EBSCOHost Database.

Cameron, K.S. & Quinn, R.E. (2011). *Diagnosing and Changing Organizational Culture Based on the Competing Values Framework.* San Francisco, CA: Jossey-Bass

Canton, J. (2007). *The Extreme Future: The Top Trends That Will Reshape the World for the Next 5, 10, and 20 Years.* New York, NY: Penguin Group.

Caserta, T. (2009). Conversing at the core: Spiritual direction and the formation of conscience. *Seminary Journal*, 15(3), 7-11. Retrieved [Accessed on October 5, 2016] from EBSCOHost Database.

Ching-Hsiang, L. (2010). Leadership: Qualities, skills, and efforts. *Interbeing*, 4(2), 19-25. Retrieved [Accessed on November 14, 2016] from EBSCOHost Database.

Ciulla, J.B., editor. (2004). *Ethics, the Heart of Leadership*, 2nd ed. Westport, CT: Praeger

Clawson, J.G. (2009). *Level Three Leadership*, 4th ed. Upper Saddle River, NJ: Pearson Prentice Hall.

Cleveland, J. (1981) I don't feel no ways tired. Retrieved from All the Lyrics Website at http://www.allthelyrics.com/lyrics/james_cleveland/i_dont_feel_no_ways_tired-lyrics-1039823.html

Coffey, J. (2015, December 24). How do magnets work. Retrieved from *Universe Today* Website at http://www.universetoday.com/82049/how-do-magnets-work/

Cohick, L.H. (2015). The real woman at the well: We know her as an adulterer and divorcée: Her community would have known otherwise. *Christianity Today*, 59(8), 66-69. Retrieved [Accessed on October 17, 2016] from EBSCOHost Database.

Davila, T., Epstein, M., & Shelton, R. (2006). *Making Innovation Work*. Upper Saddle River, NJ: Wharton School Publishing.

DeBow, G. (1990). Personal conversation.

Denning, S. (2007). *The Secret Language of Leadership*. San Francisco, CA: John Wiley & Sons, Inc.

DeSilva, D.A. (2004). *An Introduction to the New Testament: Contexts, Methods, & Ministry* Formation. Downers Grove, IL: InterVarsity Press.

DeSteno, D. (2014). *The Truth About Trust*. New York, NY: Penguin.

Dickson, E.S., Gordon, S.C. & Huber, G.A. (2015). Institutional sources of legitimate authority: An experimental investigation. *American Journal of Political Science*, 59(1), 109-127. doi:10.1111/ajps.12139

Dispensationalism. (n.d.). Retrieved from Theopedia Website at http://www.theopedia.com/dispensationalism

Doe, R., Ndinguri, E., & Phipps, S.A. (2015). Emotional intelligence: The link to success and failure of leadership. *Academy of Educational Leadership Journal*, 19(3), 105-114. Retrieved [Accessed on November 10, 2016] from EBSCOHost Database.

Duvall, J.S. & Hays, J.D. (2012). *Grasping God's Word: A Hands-On Approach to Reading, Interpreting, and Applying the Bible*, 3rd ed. Grand Rapids, MI: Zondervan Publishing.

Egan, A. (2010). Conscience, spirit, discernment: The Holy Spirit, the spiritual exercises and the formation of moral conscience. *Journal of Theology for Southern Africa, 138*57-70. Retrieved [Accessed on October 7, 2016] from EBSCOHost Database.

Fedler, K.D. (2006). *Exploring Christian Ethics: Biblical Foundations for Morality.* Westminster: John Knox Press.

Froschheiser, L. (2014). Be a passion maker: Become an accountability leader and inspire your team to exceed its goals. *Supervision,* 75(10), 15-17. Retrieved [Accessed on November 13, 2016] from EBSCOHost Database.

Fusco, T., O'Riordan, S., & Palmer, S. (2015). Authentic leaders are... conscious, competent, confident, and congruent: A grounded theory of group coaching and authentic leadership development. *International Coaching Psychology Review,* 10(2), 131-148. Retrieved [Accessed on November 10, 2016] from EBSCOHost Database.

Gardner, C. (2014). Career crossroads. *TD: Talent Development,* 68(9), 38-41. Retrieved [Accessed on November 12, 2016] from EBSCOHost Database.

Gentilman, R., & Nelson, B. (1983). Futuring: The process and implications for Training & Development practitioners.

Training & Development Journal, 37(6), 30. Retrieved [Accessed on November 11, 2016] from EBSCOHost Database.

Got questions (2016). Retrieved from http://www.gotquestions.org/Bible-virginity.html

Goudreau, J. (2012). How to tame your inner control freak. *Forbes.Com*, 20. Retrieved [Accessed on November 13, 2016] from EBSCOHost Database

Greenleaf, R. (2008). *The Servant as Leader*. Westfield, IN: The Greenleaf Center for Servant Leadership.

Hackman, M.Z. & Johnson, C.E. (2013). *Leadership: A Communication Perspective*, 6th ed. Long Grove, IL: Waveland Press, Inc.

Hamel, G. (2002). *Leading the Revolution*. New York, NY: Plume.

Harrison, S.L. (2013, February). The dishwasher king. *The Midnight Freemasons*. Retrieved from http://www.midnightfreemasons.org/2013/02/the-dishwasher-king.html

Hartman, L.P. & DesJardins, J. (2008). *Business Ethics: Decision Making for Personal Integrity & Social Responsibility*, 2nd ed., New York, NY: McGraw-Hill Irvin

Heck, P. L. (2014). Conscience across cultures: the case of Islam. *The Journal of Religion*, 94(3), 292-324. Retrieved [Accessed on October 7, 2016] from EBSCOHost Database.

Hoekstra, B. (n.d.) The grace of God. Retrieved from Blue Letter Bible Website at https://www.blueletterbible.org/Comm/hoekstra_bob/grace/grace02.cfm?a=998016

Hofstede, G., Hofstede, G.J., Minkov, M. (2010). *Cultures and Organizations: Software of the Mind*, 3rd ed. New York, NY: McGraw Hall.

Homer. (2014). *Odyssey* (Kindle Location 3996). Harper Collins Canada: Kindle Edition.

Honiball, G., Geldenhuys, D., & Mayer, C. (2014). Acknowledging others as 'whole beings': Managers' perceptions of spirituality and health in the South African workplace. *International Review of Psychiatry*, 26(3), 289-301. doi:10.3109/09540261.2014.881331

Hubbard, D.W. (2014). *How to Measure Anything*, 3rd ed., Hoboken, NJ: Wiley Press

Hughes R. L., & Beatty, K.C. (2005). *Becoming a Strategic Leader: Your Role in Your Organization's Enduring Success*. San Francisco, CA: Jossey-Bass.

Hyde, W.D. (1892). *Practical Ethics*. Rahway, NJ: The Mershon Company Press. Kindle Edition.

Jackson, B.S. (2013). On the values of biblical law and their contemporary application. *Political Theology*, 14(5), 602-618. doi:10.1179/1462317X13Z.00000000038

Jordan, S. & Hartwig, M. (2013). On the phenomenology of innocence: The role of belief in a just world. *Psychiatry, Psychology & Law*, 20(5), 749-760. doi:10.1080/13218719.2012.730903

Kalin, P., & Vichita Vathanophas, R. (2016). Knowledge creation aiding family business succession plan. *International Journal of Business & Management Science*, 6(1), 63-84. Retrieved [Accessed on October 10, 2016] from EBSCOHost Database.

Kanitz, L. (2005). Improving Christian worldview pedagogy: Going beyond mere Christianity. *Christian Higher Education*, 4(2), 99-108. doi:10.1080/15363750590923101

Keiter, S. T. (2013). Outsmarting God: Egyptian slavery and the Tower of Babel. *Jewish Bible Quarterly*, 41(3), 200-204.

Retrieved [Accessed on October 6, 2016] from
EBSCOHost Database

Khan, M.W. (n.d.). *Ramadan the Month of Fasting: Islamic Books
on the Quran, the Hadith and the Prophet Muhammad.*
Goodword Books. Kindle Edition.

Kouzes, J.M. & Posner, B. Z. (2011). Leadership begins with an
inner journey. *Leader to Leader*, 2011(60), 22-27.
doi:10.1002/ltl.464

Kuhn, T.S. (2012). *The Structure of Scientific Revolutions.*
Chicago, IL: University of Chicago Press.

Kuyper, A. (2011). *Wisdom & Wonder: Common Grace in
Science & Art* (Kindle Locations 573-574). Christian's
Library Press: Kindle Edition.

Lakota (Sioux) Culture – Four Directions. (n.d.) Retrieved from
the St. Joseph Indian School Website at
http://www.stjo.org/site/News2?page=NewsArticle&id=56
73

Leonard, D. (1998). *Wellsprings of Knowledge*. Boston, MA:
Harvard Business School Press.

Lewis, C.S. (1952). *Mere Christianity*. New York, NY: Harper
Collins Publishers.

Lingenfelter, S.G. (2008). *Leading Cross-Culturally: Covenant Relationships for Effective Christian Leadership*. Grand Rapids, MI: Baker Publishing.

Lizar, A.A., Mangundjaya, W.H., & Rachmawan, A. (2015). The role of psychological capital and psychological empowerment on individual readiness for change. *Journal of Developing Areas*, 49(5), 343-352. Retrieved [Accessed on November 10, 2016] from EBSCOHost Database.

Losey, M, Meisinger, S., & Ulrich, D.. (2005). *The Future of Human Resource Management*. Hoboken, NJ: John Wiley & Sons, Inc.

Martin, A., Woods, M., & Dawkins, S. (2016). Managing mental health in the workplace. *Rotman Management*, 74-79. Retrieved [Accessed on November 11, 2016] from EBSCOHost Database.

Mathew, M., & Gupta, K.S. (2015). Transformational leadership: Emotional intelligence. *SCMS Journal of Indian Management*, 12(2), 75-89. Retrieved [Accessed on November 9, 2016] from EBSCOHost Database.

Maxwell, J.C. (2015). *The Complete 101 Collection: What Every Leader Needs to Know*. Nashville, TN: Nelson Books.

Michalko, M. (2006). *Thinkertoys*. Berkley, CA: Ten Speed Press.

Millett, S.M. (2011). Five principles of futuring. *Futurist, 45*(5), 39-41. Retrieved [Accessed on November 11, 2016] from EBSCOHost Database.

Moos R. H. (2012). Iatrogenic effects of psychosocial interventions: Treatment, life context, and personal risk factors. *Substance Use & Misuse, 47*(13/14), 1592-1598. doi:10.3109/10826084.2012.705710

Mullen, K. (2016). Distribution of the earth's water. Retrieved from The Groundwater Association Website at http://www.ngwa.org/Fundamentals/teachers/Pages/inform ation-on-earth-water.aspx

Nantz, D.P. (2015). Exposing the roots of external control psychology: Altruism as moral compulsion. *International Journal of Choice Theory & Reality Therapy, 34*(2), 24-34. Retrieved [Accessed on October 18, 2016] from EBSCOHost Database.

Northouse, P. G. (2013). *Leadership Theory and Practice.* Thousand Oaks, CA, Sage.

Nye, B. (2014, December 15). *Bill Nye and Magnetism.* Retrieved [Accessed on October 15, 2016] from YouTube at https://youtu.be/_VwvIfmm1OE

Oster, G. (2011). *The Light Prize: Perspectives on Christian Innovation*. Virginia Beach, VA: Positive Signs Media. Kindle Edition.

Owens, B.P., & Hekman, D.R. (2016). How does leader humility influence team performance? Exploring the mechanisms of contagion and collective promotion focus. *Academy of Management Journal*, 59(3), 1088-1111. doi:10.5465/amj.2013.0660

Paul, R. & Elder, L. (2006). *Critical Thinking: Learn the Tools the Best Thinkers Use*. Upper Saddle River, NJ: Pearson Prentice Hall.

Pearson, G. (2011, October 9). African famine: "I see you." Retrieved from *Huffington Post* Website at http://www.huffingtonpost.ca/glen-pearson/africa-famine_b_922063.html

Pfeffer, J. & Sutton, R.I. (2000). The Knowing-Doing Gap. Boston, MA: Harvard Business School Press.

Reid, C. A., Davis, J.L, & Green, J.D. (2013). The Power of Change: Interpersonal Attraction as a Function of Attitude Similarity and Attitude Alignment. *Journal of Social Psychology*, 153(6), 700-719. doi:10.1080/00224545.2013.824404

Reid, W. S. (1981) The kingdom of God: the key to history. *Fides Et Historia*, 13(2), 6-15. Retrieved from EBSCOHost Database.

Regenstrief Medical Record System (RMRS) (USA). (2016). Retrieved from Bridge to Data Website at http://www.bridgetodata.org/node/1183

Robbins, S.P., & Judge, T.A. (2010). *Essentials of Organizational Behavior*. Upper Saddle River, NJ: Prentice Hall.

Robbins, V.K. (1996). *Exploring the Texture of Texts: A Guide to Socio-Rhetorical Interpretation*. Harrisburg, PA: Trinity Press International.

Rogness, M. (2012). Humor in the Bible. *Word & World*, 32(2), 117-123. Retrieved [Accessed on November 13, 2016] from EBSCOHost Database.

Rolfe, D. J. (1985). Preparing the previously married for second marriage. *The Journal of Pastoral Care*, 39(2), 110-119. Retrieved [Accessed on October 5, 2016] from EBSCOHost Database.

Ross, M. (1987). *The Fountain and the Furnace: The Way of Tears and Fire*. New York, NY: Paulist Press.

Rossant, M.J. (1966). An end to innocence. *Challenge* (05775132), 14(3), 29-32. Retrieved [Accessed on October 22, 2016] from EBSCOHost Database.

Rothwell, W.J. (2010). *Effective Succession Planning*, 4th ed. New York, NY: American Management Association.

Rothwell, W.J., Stavros, J.M., Sullivan, R.L., & Sullivan, A. (2010). *Practicing Organizational Development*, 3rd ed. San Francisco, CA: John Wiley & Sons, Inc.

Rothwell, W.J., Stavros, J.M, & Sullivan, R.L. (2016). *Practicing Organization Development*, 4th ed. Hoboken, NJ: John Wiley & Sons, Inc.

Ryrie, C.C. (1966). *Dispensationalism*. Chicago, IL: Moody Publishers. Kindle Edition.

Saving Mr. Banks. (2014). Retrieved from Walt Disney Website at http://movies.disney.com/saving-mr-banks/about

Schrage, M. (2000). *Serious Play: How the World's Best Companies Simulate to Innovate*. Boston, MA: Harvard Business School Press.

Schumm, L. (2014, June 2). The wartime origins of the M&M. Retrieved from The History Channel website at http://www.history.com/news/hungry-history/the-wartime-origins-of-the-mm

Senge, P., Kleiner, A., Roberts, C., Ross, R.B., & Smith, B.J. (1994). *The Fifth Discipline Fieldbook*. New York, NY: Crown Business.

Sharma, S.K., & Sharma, S. (2015). Psychological capital as a predictor of workplace behavior. *Journal of Management Research* (09725814), 15(1), 60-70. Retrieved [Accessed on November 10, 2016] from EBSCOHost Database.

Smiley, T. (2011). *Fail Up*. New York, NY: Hay House. Kindle Edition

Smith, H. (1991). The World's Religions. New York, NY: Harper Collins Publishers.

Spitzer, R. (2008). Wise counsel leadership. *Leadership Excellence Essentials*, 25(2), 20. Retrieved [Accessed on November 13, 2016] from EBSCOHost Database.

Sproul, R.C. (n.d.) What is grace? Retrieved from Ligonier Ministries Website at http://www.ligonier.org/learn/articles/what-grace/

Statistics on Literacy. (2015). Retrieved from United Nations Educational, Scientific, and Culture Organization Website at http://www.unesco.org/new/en/education/themes/education -building-blocks/literacy/resources/statistics

Stinton, D.B. (2013). Encountering Jesus at the well: further
    reflections on African women's Christologies. *Journal of
    Reformed Theology*, 7(3), 267-293. doi:10.1163/15697312-
    12341309

Suárez, S.A. *(2015). Effects of spirituality in the workplace. Allied
    Academies International Conference: Proceedings of The
    Academy of Organizational Culture, Communications &
    Conflict (AOCCC), 20(1), 9-13.* Retrieved [Accessed on
    October 6, 2016] from EBSCOHost Database.

The five customer segments of technology adaptation. (2016).
    Retrieved from Digital Marketing Website at
    http://www.ondigitalmarketing.com/learn/odm/foundations/
    5-customer-segments-technology-adoption/

The 5 generations in the workforce. (2016, February 19).
    Retrieved from Diversified Services Website at
    http://www.ddiversified.com/2016/02/19/the-5-generations-
    in-the-workplace/

The Wizard of Oz (1939). *Film Mate Review* retrieved from
    http://www.filmsite.org/wiza2.html

Turner, L.E. (2000, September 29). Today's ethics yield
    tomorrow's behavior. Speech retrieved from Security and

Exchange Commission's Website at
https://www.sec.gov/news/speech/spch427.htm

US Olympic team works on art of passing baton. (2008, August 7).
Retrieved from *Team USA* website at
http://www.teamusa.org/USA-Track-and-
Field/Features/2008/August/07/US-Olympic-team-works-
on-art-of-passing-the-baton

Vance, C.M., Groves, K., & Yongsun, P. (2004). Measuring and
building linear/nonlinear thinking style balance for
enhanced performance. *Academy of Management
Proceedings*, F1-F6. doi:10.5465/AMBPP.2004.13862739

Vance, C.M., Groves, K., Yongsun, P., & Kindler, H. (2007).
Understanding and measuring linear--nonlinear thinking
style for enhanced management education and professional
practice. *Academy of Management Learning & Education*,
6(2), 167-185. doi:10.5465/AMLE.2007.25223457

Van Velsor, E., McCauley, C.D., & Ruderman, M.N. (2010).
Handbook of Leadership Development, 3rd ed. San
Francisco, CA: Jossey-Bass.

Von Stiegel, H. (2011). *The Mountain Within: Leadership Lessons
and Inspiration for your Climb to the Top*. New York, NY:
McGraw Hill.

Who were the Samaritans and why were they important? (2016).
Retrieved from Catholic Answers website at
http://www.catholic.com/quickquestions/who-were-the-
samaritans-and-why-were-they-important

Wilkins, M.M. (2014). Signs that you're a micromanager. *Harvard Business Review Digital Articles*, 2-5. Retrieved [Accessed on November 14, 2016] from EBSCOHost Database.

Willard, D. (1998). Spiritual disciplines, spiritual formation, and the restoration of the soul. *Journal of Psychology & Theology*, 26(1), 101-109.

Witherington, B. III. (2011). *Work: A Kingdom Perspective on Labor*. Grand Rapids, MI: William B. Eerdmans Publishing Company.

Woods, K. (2016). Organizational ambidexterity and the multi-generational workforce. *Journal of Organizational Culture, Communications & Conflict*, 20(1), 95-111. Retrieved [Accessed on October 13, 2016] from EBSCOHost Database.

Zou, T. & Lee, W.B. (2010). A study of the similarity in mental models and team performance. *Proceedings of The International Conference on Intellectual Capital, Knowledge Management & Organizational Learning*, 536-

544. Retrieved [Accessed on October 6, 2016] from
EBSCOHost Database.

i Michael Rogness. (2012). Humor in the Bible. *Word & World*, 32(2), 117-123.
Retrieved [Accessed on November 13, 2016] from EBSCOHost Database.
ii Huston Smith. (1991). *The World's Religions.* New York, NY: Harper Collins
Publishers.
iii Lakota (Sioux) Culture – Four Directions. (n.d.) Retrieved from the St. Joseph
Indian School Website at
http://www.stjo.org/site/News2?page=NewsArticle&id=5673
iv Dispensationalism. (n.d.). Retrieved from *Theopedia* Website at
http://www.theopedia.com/dispensationalism
v W. Stanford Reid, (1981). The kingdom of God: the key to history. *Fides Et
Historia*, 13(2), 6-15. Retrieved from EBSCOHost Database.
vi Ibid., p. 40.
vii Diane B. Stinton, (2013). Encountering Jesus at the well: further reflections
on African women's Christologies. *Journal of Reformed Theology*, 7(3), 267-
293. doi:10.1163/15697312-12341309
viii Vernon K. Robbins, (1996) *Exploring the Texture of Texts: A Guide to Socio-
Rhetorical Interpretation.* Harrisburg, PA: Trinity Press International.
ix Ibid., p. 7.
x Ibid., p. 40.
xi Ibid., p. 95.
xii Chelsea A. Reid, Jodie L. Davis, & Jeffrey D. Green, (2013). The Power of
Change: Interpersonal Attraction as a Function of Attitude Similarity and
Attitude Alignment. *Journal of Social Psychology*, 153(6), 700-719.
doi:10.1080/00224545.2013.824404
xiii Who were the Samaritans and why were they important? (2016). Retrieved
from Catholic Answers website at
http://www.catholic.com/quickquestions/who-were-the-samaritans-and-why-
were-they-important

[xiv] James M. Kouzes, & Barry Z. Posner, (2011). Leadership begins with an inner journey. *Leader to Leader*, 2011(60), 22-27. doi:10.1002/ltl.464

[xv] Genevieve DeBow, personal conversation, 1990.

[xvi] Lee Froschheiser. (2014). Be a passion maker: Become an accountability leader and inspire your team to exceed its goals. *Supervision*, 75(10), 15-17. Retrieved [Accessed on November 13, 2016] from EBSCOHost Database.

[xvii] *The Wizard of Oz* (1939). Film Mate Review retrieved from http://www.filmsite.org/wiza2.html

[xviii] Richard Paul & Linda Elder. (2006). *Critical Thinking: Learn the Tools the Best Thinkers Use*. Upper Saddle River, NJ: Pearson Prentice Hall.

[xix] Ibid., p. 84.

[xx] Ibid., p. 89.

[xxi] Sarah Jordan, & Maria Hartwig. (2013). On the phenomenology of innocence: The role of belief in a just world. *Psychiatry, Psychology & Law*, 20(5), 749-760. doi:10.1080/13218719.2012.730903

[xxii] Peter Senge, Art Kleiner, Charlotte Roberts, Richard B. Ross, & Bryan J. Smith. (1994). *The Fifth Discipline Fieldbook*. New York, NY: Crown Business.

[xxiii] Ibid., p. 6.

[xxiv] Ibid., p. 49.

[xxv] Charles, M. Vance, Kevin Groves, Paik Yongsun, & Herb Kindler. (2007). Understanding and measuring linear--nonlinear thinking style for enhanced management education and professional practice. *Academy of Management Learning & Education*, 6(2), 167-185. doi:10.5465/AMLE.2007.25223457

[xxvi] Ibid., p. 169.

[xxvii] http://www.gotquestions.org/Bible-virginity.html

[xxviii] Business Utopia (blog) retrieved from https://www.businesstopia.net/communication/psychological-barriers on October 5, 2016.

[xxix] DeSteno, D. (2014). *The Truth About Trust*. New York, NY: Penguin.

[xxx] Ibid., p. 16

[xxxi] Gary Hamel. (2002). *Leading the Revolution*. New York, NY: Plume.

[xxxii] Michael Michalko. (2006). *Thinkertoys*. Berkley, CA: Ten Speed Press.

[xxxiii] Ibid., p. xv.

[xxxiv] Tony Davila, Marc J. Epstein, & Robert Shelton. (2006). *Making Innovation Work*. Upper Saddle River, NJ: Wharton School Publishing.

[xxxv] James G. Clawson. (2009). *Level Three Leadership*, 4th ed. Upper Saddle River, NJ: Pearson Prentice Hall.

[xxxvi] William J. Rothwell, Jacqueline M. Stavros, & Roland L. Sullivan. (2016). *Practicing Organization Development*, 4th ed. Hoboken, NJ: John Wiley & Sons, Inc.

xxxvii Ibid., Kindle Location 1035.

xxxviii Michael Losey, Sue Meisinger, & Dave Ulrich. (2005). *The Future of Human Resource Management*. Hoboken, NJ: John Wiley & Sons, Inc.

xxxix Ibid., p. 158.

xl Sarah Ban Breathnach. (2005). *Simple Abundance*. New York, NY: Grand Central Publishing.

xli Thomas Caserta. (2009). Conversing at the Core: Spiritual Direction and the Formation of Conscience. *Seminary Journal*, 15(3), 7-11. Retrieved [Accessed on October 5, 2016] from EBSCOHost Database.

xlii Richard Paul & Linda Elder. (2006). *Critical Thinking: Learn the Tools the Best Thinkers Use*. Upper Saddle River, NJ: Pearson Prentice Hall.

xliii Ibid., p. 91.

xliv Kyle D. Fedler. (2006). Exploring Christian Ethics: Biblical Foundations for Morality, Westminster John Knox Press.

xlv Richard Paul & Linda Elder (2006). *Critical Thinking: Learn the Tools the Best Thinkers Use*. Upper Saddle River, NJ: Pearson Prentice Hall.

xlvi David J. Rolfe. (1985). Preparing the previously married for second marriage. *The Journal of Pastoral Care*, 39(2), 110-119. Retrieved [Accessed on October 5, 2016] from EBSCOHost Database.

xlvii William J. Rothwell. (2010). *Effective Succession Planning*, 4th ed. New York, NY: American Management Association.

xlviii Ben Witherington III. (2011). *Work: A Kingdom Perspective on Labor*. Grand Rapids, MI: William B. Eerdmans Publishing Company.

xlix Ibid., p. 104.

l Ibid., p. 117.

li Dallas Willard. (1998). Spiritual disciplines, spiritual formation, and the restoration of the soul. *Journal of Psychology & Theology*, 26(1), 101-109

lii Ibid., p. 103.

liii Shirley A. Suárez. (2015). Effects of spirituality in the workplace. *Allied Academies International Conference: Proceedings of The Academy of Organizational Culture, Communications & Conflict* (AOCCC), 20(1), 9-13. Retrieved [Accessed on October 6, 2016] from EBSCOHost Database.

liv Paul L. Heck. (2014). Conscience across cultures: the case of Islam. *The Journal of Religion*, 94(3), 292-324. Retrieved [Accessed on October 7, 2016] from EBSCOHost Database.

lv George Honiball, Derk Geldenhuys, & Claude-Helene Mayer. (2014). Acknowledging others as 'whole beings': Managers' perceptions of spirituality and health in the South African workplace. *International Review of Psychiatry*, 26(3), 289-301. doi:10.3109/09540261.2014.881331

[lvi] Kathryn Woods. (2016). Organizational ambidexterity and the multi-generational workforce. *Journal of Organizational Culture, Communications & Conflict*, 20(1), 95-111. Retrieved [Accessed on October 13, 2016] from EBSCOHost Database.

[lvii] Ibid., p. 295.

[lviii] Anthony Egan. (2010). Conscience, spirit, discernment: The Holy Spirit, the spiritual exercises and the formation of moral conscience. *Journal of Theology for Southern Africa*, 13857-70. Retrieved [Accessed on October 7, 2016] from EBSCOHost Database.

[lix] Bill Nye. (2014, December 15). *Bill Nye and Magnetism*. Retrieved [Accessed on October 15, 2016] from YouTube at https://youtu.be/_VwvIfmm1OE

[lx] Ibid., pp. 46-47.

[lxi] Matthew R. Auer. (2011). The policy sciences of social media. *Policy Studies Journal*, 39(4), 709-736. doi:10.1111/j.1541-0072.2011.00428.x

[lxii] Lori Kanitz. (2005). Improving Christian worldview pedagogy: Going beyond mere Christianity. *Christian Higher Education*, 4(2), 99-108. doi:10.1080/15363750590923101

[lxiii] Rothwell, W.J., Stavros, J.M., Sullivan, R.L., & Sullivan, A. (2010). Practicing Organizational Development, 3rd ed. San Francisco, CA: John Wiley & Sons, Inc.

[lxiv] Charles C. Ryrie. (1966). *Dispensationalism*. Chicago, IL: Moody Publishers. Kindle Edition.

[lxv] Chantal Gardner. (2014). Career crossroads. *TD: Talent Development*, 68(9), 38-41. Retrieved [Accessed on November 12, 2016] from EBSCOHost Database.

[lxvi] Sheila T. Keiter. (2013). Outsmarting God: Egyptian slavery and the Tower of Babel. *Jewish Bible Quarterly*, 41(3), 200-204. Retrieved [Accessed on October 6, 2016] from EBSCOHost Database.

[lxvii] Ibid., p. 204.

[lxviii] Morag Barrett. (2014). Are you a Control Freak?. *Leadership Excellence Essentials*, 31(3), 28-29. Retrieved [Accessed on November 13, 2016] from EBSCOHost Database.

[lxix] Ibid., p. 28.

[lxx] Jenna Goudreau. (2012). How to tame your inner control freak. *Forbes.Com*, 20. Retrieved [Accessed on November 14, 2016] from EBSCOHost Database.

[lxxi] Muriel M. Wilkins. (2014). Signs that you're a micromanager. *Harvard Business Review Digital Articles*, 2-5. Retrieved [Accessed on November 14, 2016] from EBSCOHost Database.

[lxxii] Herta Von Stiegel. (2011). *The Mountain Within: Leadership Lessons and Inspiration for your Climb to the Top*. New York, NY: McGraw Hill.

[lxxiii] *Saving Mr. Banks*. (2014). Retrieved from Walt Disney Website at http://movies.disney.com/saving-mr-banks/about

[lxxiv] Randy Spitzer. (2008). Wise counsel leadership. *Leadership Excellence Essentials*, 25(2), 20. Retrieved [Accessed on November 13, 2016] from EBSCOHost Database.

[lxxv] Geert Hofstede, Gert J. Hofstede, & Michael Minkov. (2010). *Cultures and Organizations: Software of the Mind*, 3rd ed. New York, NY: McGraw Hall.

[lxxvi] Ibid., p. 448.

[lxxvii] Ibid., p. 464

[lxxviii] Tracy Zou, & W.B. Lee. (2010). A study of the similarity in mental models and team performance. *Proceedings of The International Conference on Intellectual Capital, Knowledge Management & Organizational Learning*, 536-544. Retrieved [Accessed on October 6, 2016] from EBSCOHost Database.

[lxxix] Rudolf H. Moos. (2012). Iatrogenic effects of psychosocial interventions: Treatment, life context, and personal risk factors. *Substance Use & Misuse*, 47(13/14), 1592-1598. doi:10.3109/10826084.2012.705710

[lxxx] William J. Rothwell, Jacqueline M. Stavros, Roland L. Sullivan, & Arielle Sullivan. (2010). *Practicing Organizational Development*, 3rd ed. San Francisco, CA: John Wiley & Sons, Inc.

[lxxxi] Michael Schrage. (2000). *Serious Play: How the World's Best Companies Simulate to Innovate*. Boston, MA: Harvard Business School Press.

[lxxxii] Ibid., p. 89.

[lxxxiii] Thomas S. Kuhn (2012). *The Structure of Scientific Revolutions*. Chicago, IL: University of Chicago Press.

[lxxxiv] Ibid., p. 137.

[lxxxv] Eric S. Dickson, Sanford C. Gordon, & Gregory A. Huber. (2015). Institutional sources of legitimate authority: An experimental investigation. *American Journal of Political Science*, 59(1), 109-127. doi:10.1111/ajps.12139

[lxxxvi] Clarence A. Beckwith. (1911). The types of authority in Christian belief. *Harvard Theological Review*, 4(2), 241-252. Retrieved [Accessed on November 9, 2016] from EBSCOHost Database.

[lxxxvii] Sherri Brown. (2015). What Is truth? Jesus, Pilate, and the staging of the dialogue of the cross in John 18:28-19:16a. *The Catholic Biblical Quarterly*, 77(1), 69-86. Retrieved [Accessed on November 13, 2016] from EBSCOHost Database.

[lxxxviii] Glen Pearson. (2011, October 9). African famine: "I see you." Retrieved from *Huffington Post* Website at http://www.huffingtonpost.ca/glen-pearson/africa-famine_b_922063.html

lxxxixAyu A. Lizar, Wustari H. Mangundjaya, & Ahmad Rachmawan. (2015). The role of psychological capital and psychological empowerment on individual readiness for change. *Journal of Developing Areas*, 49(5), 343-352. Retrieved [Accessed on November 10, 2016] from EBSCOHost Database.

xc Sanjeev K. Sharma, & Shikha Sharma. (2015). Psychological capital as a predictor of workplace behavior. *Journal of Management Research* (09725814), 15(1), 60-70. Retrieved [Accessed on November 10, 2016] from EBSCOHost Database.

xci Dorothy Leonard. (1998). *Wellsprings of Knowledge*. Boston, MA: Harvard Business School Press.

xcii Nancy E. Adams. (2015). Bloom's taxonomy of cognitive learning objectives. *Journal of The Medical Library Association*, 103(3), 152-153. doi:10.3163/1536-5050.103.3.010

xciii Peter Senge, Art Kleiner, Charlotte Roberts, Richard B. Ross, & Bryan J. Smith. (1994). *The Fifth Discipline Fieldbook*. New York, NY: Crown Business.

xciv Ibid., p. 199.

xcv Charles C. Ryrie. (1966). *Dispensationalism*. Chicago, IL: Moody Publishers. Kindle Edition.

xcvi Lynn E. Turner. (2000, September 29). Today's ethics yield tomorrow's behavior. Speech retrieved from Security and Exchange Commission's Website at https://www.sec.gov/news/speech/spch427.htm

xcvii Stephen P. Robbins, & Timothy A. Judge. (2010). *Essentials of Organizational Behavior*. Upper Saddle River, NJ: Prentice Hall.

xcviii Ibid., p. 124.

xcix Michael Blanding. (2015, January 26). Workplace stress responsible for up to $190 billion in annual U.S. healthcare costs. Retrieved from *Forbes* Website at http://www.forbes.com/sites/hbsworkingknowledge/2015/01/26/workplace-stress-responsible-for-up-to-190-billion-in-annual-u-s-heathcare-costs/#19bbce2d4333

c Angela Martin, Megan Woods, & Sarah Dawkins (2016). Managing mental health in the workplace. *Rotman Management*, 74-79. Retrieved [Accessed on November 11, 2016] from EBSCOHost Database.

ci Ibid., p. 78.

cii Peter G. Northouse. (2013). Leadership Theory and Practice. Thousand Oaks, CA, Sage.

ciii Molly Mathew, & K.S. Gupta. (2015). Transformational leadership: Emotional intelligence. *SCMS Journal of Indian Management*, 12(2), 75-89. Retrieved [Accessed on November 9, 2016] from EBSCOHost Database.

civ Ibid., p. 248.

[cv] Robert Greenleaf. (2008). *The Servant as Leader*. Westfield, IN: The Greenleaf Center for Servant Leadership.

[cvi] Tony Fusco, Siobhain O'Riordan, & Stephen Palmer. (2015). Authentic leaders are... conscious, competent, confident, and congruent: A grounded theory of group coaching and authentic leadership development. *International Coaching Psychology Review*, 10(2), 131-148. Retrieved [Accessed on November 10, 2016] from EBSCOHost Database.

[cvii] Joanne B. Ciulla, editor. (2004). *Ethics, the Heart of Leadership*, 2nd ed. Westport, CT: Praeger.

[cviii] Ibid., p. 95.

[cix] Laura P. Hartman & Joe DesJardins. (2008). *Business Ethics: Decision Making for Personal Integrity & Social Responsibility*, 2nd ed., New York, NY: McGraw-Hill Irvin.

[cx] Homer. (2014). *Odyssey* (Kindle Location 3996). Harper Collins Canada: Kindle Edition.

[cxi] Bradley P. Owens, & David R. Hekman. (2016). How does leader humility influence team performance? Exploring the mechanisms of contagion and collective promotion focus. *Academy of Management Journal*, 59(3), 1088-1111. doi:10.5465/amj.2013.0660

[cxii] Raymond Doe, Erastus Ndinguri, & Simone A. Phipps. (2015). Emotional intelligence: The link to success and failure of leadership. *Academy of Educational Leadership Journal*, 19(3), 105-114. Retrieved [Accessed on November 10, 2016] from EBSCOHost Database.

[cxiii] Ibid., p. 106.

[cxiv] Jerry Coffey. (2015, December 24). How do magnets work. Retrieved from *Universe Today* Website at http://www.universetoday.com/82049/how-do-magnets-work/

[cxv] Bernard S. Jackson. (2013). On the values of biblical law and their contemporary application. *Political Theology*, 14(5), 602-618. doi:10.1179/1462317X13Z.00000000038

[cxvi] David A. DeSilva. (2004). *An Introduction to the New Testament: Contexts, Methods, & Ministry Formation*. Downers Grove, IL: InterVarsity Press.

[cxvii] Laura Schumm. (2014, June 2). The wartime origins of the M&M. Retrieved from *The History Channel* website at http://www.history.com/news/hungry-history/the-wartime-origins-of-the-mm

[cxviii] Lynn H. Cohick. (2015). The real woman at the well: We know her as an adulterer and divorcée: Her community would have known otherwise. *Christianity Today*, 59(8), 66-69. Retrieved [Accessed on October 17, 2016] from EBSCOHost Database.

cxix Derrick P. Nantz. (2015). Exposing the roots of external control psychology: Altruism as moral compulsion. *International Journal of Choice Theory & Reality Therapy*, 34(2), 24-34. Retrieved [Accessed on October 18, 2016] from EBSCOHost Database.

cxx Ibid., p. 26.

cxxi Edgar H. Schein. (2010). *Organizational Culture and Leadership*, 4th ed. San Francisco, CA: Jossey-Bass.

cxxii Ibid., p. 360.

cxxiii Matthew 5:17. (n.d.) Retrieved from Bible Gateway Website at https://www.biblegateway.com/passage/?search=matthew+5%3A17&version=GNV

cxxiv William J. Rothwell, Jacqueline M. Stavros, Roland L. Sullivan, & Arielle Sullivan. (2010). *Practicing Organizational Development*, 3rd ed. San Francisco, CA: John Wiley & Sons, Inc.

cxxv Ibid., p. 137.

cxxvi James G. Clawson. (2009). *Level Three Leadership: Getting Below the Surface*, 4th ed. Upper Saddle River, NJ: Pearson Prentice Hall.

cxxvii Ibid., p. 220.

cxxviii Michael Michalko. (2006). *Thinkertoys*. Berkley, CA: Ten Speed Press.

cxxix Ibid., p. 56.

cxxx Civil lawsuit statistics. (2016). Retrieved from Statistics Brain Website at http://www.statisticbrain.com/civil-lawsuit-statistics/

cxxxi James Cleveland. (1981) I don't feel no ways tired. Retrieved from All the Lyrics Website at http://www.allthelyrics.com/lyrics/james_cleveland/i_dont_feel_no_ways_tired-lyrics-1039823.html

cxxxii Bob Hoekstra. (n.d.) The grace of God. Retrieved from Blue Letter Bible Website at https://www.blueletterbible.org/Comm/hoekstra_bob/grace/grace02.cfm?a=998016

cxxxiii Nathan W. Bingham (2012, April 11). Charles Spurgeon on Calvanism – irresistible grace. Retrieved from Ligonier Ministries Website at http://www.ligonier.org/blog/charles-spurgeon-calvinism-irresistible-grace/

cxxxiv R.C. Sproul (n.d.) What is grace? Retrieved from Ligonier Ministries Website at http://www.ligonier.org/learn/articles/what-grace/

cxxxv Abraham Kuyper. (2011). *Wisdom & Wonder: Common Grace in Science & Art* (Kindle Locations 573-574). Christian's Library Press. Kindle Edition.

cxxxvi Kimberly Mullen. (2016). Distribution of the earth's water. Retrieved from The Groundwater Association Website at

http://www.ngwa.org/Fundamentals/teachers/Pages/information-on-earth-water.aspx

cxxxvii Sherri Brown. (2015). Water imagery and the power and presence of God in the Gospel of John. *Theology Today* (Online), 72(3), 289-298. doi:10.1177/0040573615601471

cxxxviiiIbid., p. 293.

cxxxix Paula Caligiuri. (2012). *Cultural Agility: Building a Pipeline of Successful Global Professionals*. San Francisco, CA: Jossey-Bass.

cxl Sherwood G. Lingenfelter. (2008). *Leading Cross-Culturally: Covenant Relationships for Effective Christian Leadership*. Grand Rapids, MI: Baker Publishing.

cxli Ibid., p. 64.

cxlii Maulana Wahiduddin Khan. (n.d.). *Ramadan the Month of Fasting: Islamic Books on the Quran, the Hadith and the Prophet Muhammad* Goodword Books. Kindle Edition.

cxliii Sherwood G. Lingenfelter. (2008). *Leading Cross-Culturally: Covenant Relationships for Effective Christian Leadership*. Grand Rapids, MI: Baker Publishing.

cxliv Angel Cabrera & Gregory Unruh. (2012). *Being Global: How to Think, Act, and Lead in a Transformed World*. Boston, MA: Harvard Business Review Press.

cxlv Ibid., p. 172.

cxlvi Michael Michalko. (2009). *Thinkertoys*. Berkley, CA: Ten Speed Press.

cxlvii Ibid., p. 244.

cxlviii Thomas S. Kuhn (2012). *The Structure of Scientific Revolutions*. Chicago, IL: University of Chicago Press.

cxlix Lexicon: Strong's G1722. (n.d.). Retrieved from Blue Letter Bible Website at https://www.blueletterbible.org/lang/lexicon/lexicon.cfm?Strongs=G1722&t=KJV

cl Ibid., n.p.

cli Maggie Ross. (1987). *The Fountain and the Furnace: The Way of Tears and Fire*. New York, NY: Paulist Press.

clii C.S. Lewis. (1952). *Mere Christianity*. New York, NY: Harper Collins Publishers.

cliiiPipatanantakurn Kalin, & Rachtam Vichita Vathanophas. (2016). Knowledge creation aiding family business succession plan. *International Journal of Business & Management Science*, 6(1), 63-84. Retrieved [Accessed on October 10, 2016] from EBSCOHost Database.

[cliv] US Olympic team works on art of passing baton. (2008, August 7). Retrieved from *Team USA* website at http://www.teamusa.org/USA-Track-and-Field/Features/2008/August/07/US-Olympic-team-works-on-art-of-passing-the-baton

[clv] Peter Senge, Art Kleiner, Charlotte Roberts, Richard B. Ross, & Bryan J. Smith. (1994). *The Fifth Discipline Fieldbook*. New York, NY: Crown Business.

[clvi] Ibid., p. 48.

[clvii] Ibid., p. 48.

[clviii] James Canton. (2007). *The Extreme Future: The Top Trends That Will Reshape the World for the Next 5, 10, and 20 Years*. New York, NY: Penguin Group.

[clix] Jeffrey Pfeffer & Robert I. Sutton (2000). *The Knowing-Doing Gap*. Boston, MA: Harvard Business School Press.

[clx] Tavis Smiley. (2011). *Fail Up* (Kindle Locations 2257-2258). New York, NY: Hay House. Kindle Edition.

[clxi] Thelma B. Burgonito-Watson. (2005). Sexism and racial ethnic women in the church: a reflection on the Samaritan woman. *Church & Society*, 95(4), 89-93. Retrieved [Accessed on October 17, 2016] from EBSCOHost Database.

[clxii] Michael Schrage. (2000). *Serious Play: How the World's Best Companies Simulate to Innovate*. Boston, MA: Harvard Business School Press.

[clxiii] David A. DeSilva. (2004). *An Introduction to the New Testament: Contexts, Methods, & Ministry Formation*. Downers Grove, IL: InterVarsity Press.

[clxiv] Maggie Ross. (1987). *The Fountain and the Furnace: The Way of Tears and Fire*. New York, NY: Paulist Press.

[clxv] Ibid., p. 91.

[clxvi] Ibid., p. 71.

[clxvii] Ibid., p. 48.

[clxviii] Ibid., p. 445.

[clxix] Liu Ching-Hsiang. (2010). Leadership: Qualities, skills, and efforts. *Interbeing*, 4(2), 19-25. Retrieved [Accessed on November 14, 2016] from EBSCOHost Database.

[clxx] William J. Rothwell. (2010). *Effective Succession Planning*, 4th ed. New York, NY: American Management Association.

[clxxi] Ibid., p. 252.

[clxxii] Ibid., p. 296.

[clxxiii] Gary Oster. (2011). *The Light Prize: Perspectives on Christian Innovation*. Virginia Beach, VA: Positive Signs Media. Kindle Edition.

[clxxiv] William De Witt Hyde. (1892). *Practical Ethics*. Rahway, NJ: The Mershon Company Press. Kindle Edition.

[clxxv]Steven L. Harrison. (2013, February). The dishwasher king. *The Midnight Freemasons*. Retrieved from http://www.midnightfreemasons.org/2013/02/the-dishwasher-king.html

[clxxvi] Regenstrief Medical Record System (RMRS) (USA). (2016). Retrieved from Bridge to Data Website at http://www.bridgetodata.org/node/1183

[clxxvii] Richard Paul & Linda Elder. (2006). *Critical Thinking: Learning the Best Tools the Best Thinkers Use*, concise edition. Upper Saddle River, NJ: Pearson Prentice Hall.

[clxxviii] Ibid., p. 263.

[clxxix] Ibid., p. 3.

[clxxx] John C. Maxwell. (2015). *The Complete 101 Collection: What Every Leader Needs to Know*. Nashville, TN: Nelson Books.

[clxxxi] Statistics on Literacy. (2015). Retrieved from United Nations Educational, Scientific, and Culture Organization Website at http://www.unesco.org/new/en/education/themes/education-building-blocks/literacy/resources/statistics

[clxxxii] Richard L. Hughes, & Katherine C. Beatty. (2005). *Becoming a Strategic Leader: Your Role in Your Organization's Enduring Success*. San Francisco, CA: Jossey-Bass.

[clxxxiii] Stephen M. Millett. (2011). Five principles of futuring. *Futurist, 45*(5), 39-41. Retrieved [Accessed on November 11, 2016] from EBSCOHost Database.

[clxxxiv] Ruth Gentilman, & Barbara Nelson. (1983). Futuring: The process and implications for Training & Development practitioners. *Training & Development Journal, 37*(6), 30. Retrieved [Accessed on November 11, 2016] from EBSCOHost Database.

[clxxxv] Ibid., p. 44.

[clxxxvi] James Clawson. (2009). *Level Three Leadership: Getting Below the Surface*, 4th ed. Upper Saddle River, NJ: Pearson Prentice Hall.

[clxxxvii] Chuck Callahan. (2009). Resonance, dissonance, and leadership. *U.S. Army Medical Department Journal*, 32-36. Retrieved [Accessed on November 15, 2016] from EBSCOHost Database.

[clxxxviii] Herta Von Stiegel. (2011). *The Mountain Within: Leadership Lessons and Inspiration for your Climb to the Top*. New York, NY: McGraw Hill.

www.ingramcontent.com/pod-product-compliance
Lightning Source LLC
Chambersburg PA
CBHW060154070426
42447CB00033B/1282